CREATING GREAT GRAPHIC DESIGN TO A BUDGET

PLANNING/SOURCING/DESIGNING/FINISHING

Scott Witham

ERWIN BAUER
AUSTRIA

RotoVision

CONTENTS

MICHAEL SEISER
VIENNA

INTRODUCTION

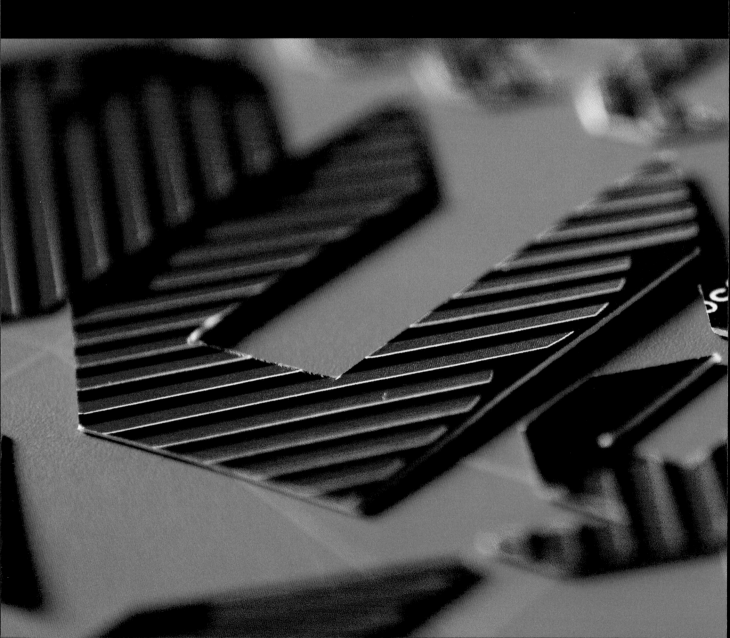

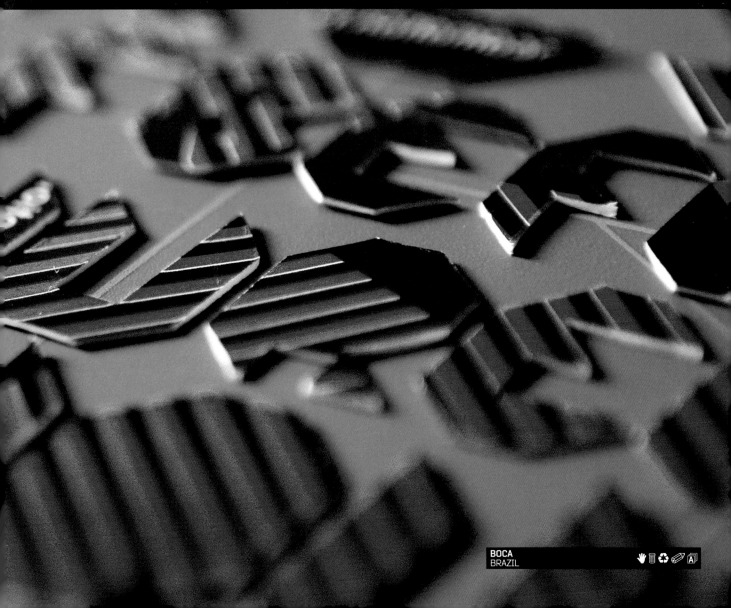

WORKING TO A BUDGET

Being asked to design to a reduced budget can strike fear into the heart of a graphic designer. But what exactly does a reduced budget mean to the result?

Does it mean the idea or the work are any less powerful, or that the message is lost due to a lack of development time? Absolutely not. If this were the case, why bother commissioning a designer at all?

For most designers, a reduced budget simply means that they look to cut the outgoing costs, but not the quality of the design. Can we do the photography in-house or source it externally? Can we do our own illustrations? Do we really need 2,000 copies of a finished 24-page, full-color brochure with spot varnishing and die-cut edges? The last thing a good designer will want to cut is the creative. A good designer should take ownership of everything they have designed, from a small flier right through to a national campaign or branding exercise. Cost can sometimes be irrelevant to how something looks and works. If a designer is involved in a peice of work, they should stand by that work.

Increasingly, designers are having to "think smarter," take what budgets they have been given and turn around fantastic pieces of work, giving the client great value for money. Truth be told, we are probably all employing this ethos on almost every job we do, every day, anyway. It's not always a case of budgets being cut; more often it's a case of clients wanting their money to go further, to feel they got a great deal on a great piece of creative. Do this and your client will come back for more, bonding your relationship and truly benefiting both parties.

Designing on a budget doesn't mean cheap design. There are many ways in which designers have reduced their costs simply through smart thinking. The budget could have been next to nothing or tens of thousands; the point is that without clever thinking, the final costs would have been so much higher.

We explore how designers employ and adapt all of their design experience and knowledge to help get the most out of what is available. How do they maximize the print budget? Is it through a clever use of folding, by using a lighter-weight paper, or by printing with two spot colors instead of full color? Did they hand-finish by folding or packing themselves? Did they use found materials, reduced-price papers, or even materials bought cheap from eBay?

**HEYDUK, MUSIL & STRNAD
CZECH REPUBLIC**

◄ This eye-catching print was achieved by overprinting two spot colors with spot gold.

In this book we will discover, explore, and reveal many tricks of the trade used by designers from all over the world. We hear directly from the creative teams, with quotes on page visuals, how the work was achieved, what finishes were used, and how they managed to save money, yet still have a fantastic end product to help generate new business and to sell on to their clients. We will also explore how to get the best from your software, your computers, typefaces, paper suppliers, even your digital cameras.

Good designers know that the value of their work is not necessarily tied to its production cost. A good idea is a good idea regardless of what money is then thrown at it. Large print budgets can enhance a good idea, but they cannot hide a bad one. A great idea will shine, even with a reduced budget.

❯ Mono newsletters with a second overprinted spot color produced for KVS (Royal Flemish Theater) in Brussels, Belgium.

COAST
BELGIUM

PRODUCTION KEY

This book showcases many different approaches to design and print, but all have one thing in common—they are examples of fantastic design without a fantastic budget.

With each example is a credit to the designer, and alongside this credit we have included icons to indicate specific elements and techniques used in the design. Not every piece of design will fall neatly into a specific section: a brochure printed with a single spot color may also be printed on colored paper or board and feature hand-folding or in-house finishing.

It is important to consider all possibilities when designing on a reduced budget. If you can save money by printing with a single spot color, can you save even more by requesting that the printer supply the finished work scored, but not folded? More often than not, if substantial savings have been made, the client will happily accept that their help may be required to complete the work. Perhaps the client may even see this as fun and a means of getting involved in the production of their own literature.

○	One spot color
◊	Two spot colors
◊◊	Three spot colors
⠒	CMYK litho
▪▪	CMYK digital
◈	Screenprinting
▤	Colored paper
Ⓐ	Alternatives to art
ABC	Budget font
A	Created font
⤥	Hand-drawn font
∂	Vector illustration

✎	Traditional illustration
✒	Digital illustration
◉	DIY photography
⤓	Stock photography
⧄	Forms & folds
▭	Paper stock
♻	Recycled
✳	Finishes
⊘	Binding
✋	In-house finishes
▦	Found material

> Eagleclean is a cleaning company targeting advertising and design agencies. The logo uses the tools of the trade to communicate the name in a simple and impactful way.

THE PARTNERS
UK

SOLAR INITIATIVE
THE NETHERLANDS

^ Solar Initiative was commissioned to create the
‹ corporate identity and communication tools for
Via Milano, an organization that promotes Dutch
Design. The solution had to be effective, creative,
and very low-cost in terms of print and artwork.

THIS BOOK
AND HOW WE CREATED IT ON A BUDGET

The main priority for this publication was to produce a book that would be an excellent source of design inspiration and supply tips on how to produce great design work to a strict budget. The next highest priority was to do this on time and with minimal financial outlay.

This book has been created using many of the tricks featured in its pages. The first task was to get design agencies from around the world to submit work. To keep artwork costs down, our Call for Entries encouraged designers to submit high-resolution files on disk to reduce the amount of photography required for this publication. The author, Scott Witham, contacted *Creative Review* (a respected design publication) and was able to secure a cancellation rate for a full-page advert. The number of projects submitted in response to this ran into the hundreds—the cost of the advert was worth every penny. Witham also promoted the Call for Entries through design blogs and forums, and contacted companies directly via e-mail. This reduced all outside costs by eliminating the need for postage and telephone calls.

In addition, Witham used paper mill account directors to help promote the work. Their job brings them into contact with countless design, advertising, and print companies—a valuable source of the work required for this book. Regional design magazines such as Scotland's *Drum* were brought in, free of charge, to run short articles on the book, and this helped to ensure that local design work was also sourced.

To keep studio costs down, Witham recruited students from local art school Duncan of Jordanstone to assist in the early scamps for cover designs, page layouts, and low-resolution positional photography.

Free fonts were sourced, copyright-free photography downloaded, and all submissions carefully pondered prior to work commencing on this book.

Once the design of the book was well underway, Traffic were able to keep costs down, as well as speed up communications, by working purely with e-mailed PDFs. Only two sets of color proofs were printed, and these were used solely by Traffic to control the pagination and as a visual guide to move projects throughout the book.

‹ Chris Smith checking proposed layouts and running order for all projects and pages.

› Designers Gordon Beveridge and Craig Gallacher bringing the book to life.

⌄ Various stages of the book's production and some of the hundreds of submissions received. Bottom right is the full-page, hand-drawn advert created for design publication *Creative Review*.

THE BASICS
YOU CAN'T AFFORD TO LIVE WITHOUT

Image sourced online from Stock.XCHNG. The photo taken by user maxray06 is one of a huge gallery of over 350,000 quality stock photos by more than 30,000 photographers.

You don't need all the very latest kit (although it does help) to produce great designs on a budget.

Graphic design did exist before the computer, but it was a much slower, more costly, and less accessible resource than it is today. The revolution that was desktop publishing has turned the world of design on its head. It has cut the cost of creating design dramatically, allowed designers to set up their own artwork and produce their own end product. Some (usually those unable to modernize and adapt) may argue that this has come at the cost of creativity, but the world marches on at a relentless rate and good design will always stand the test of time.

The industry standard for hardware is the Apple Macintosh. With their G5 towers, iMacs, and MacBooks, there is simply no substitute for the design industry. (At least you know it will dock easily with your iPod.) Sadly, there are very few bargains to be had buying a new Apple Macintosh computer; prices appear to be controlled so huge discounts on current models are very rarely found. Even outgoing models are only discounted by a small amount. Buying secondhand or on eBay is a risk. Why is it there? Why is it so cheap? If it seems too good to be true, it usually is. Buying a refurbished computer from a reputable source can often get you the safest deals, as your computer will come with a warranty. Make sure you buy from an honest, reputable dealer with someone you can speak to if things go wrong.

Unfortunately, the same rules apply to software. With so many upgrades and new versions being released, investment in software is unavoidable. Maintaining reasonably up-to-date software will keep you designing efficiently—just don't expect the software to generate good ideas for you. Files created with really old software may be rejected as soon as they are received. Clients cannot review files they can't open, and printers cannot print them. Secondhand software can often be difficult to install, especially if it has already been registered; you might need to apply for new registration codes, and these may not be given.

Always shop around for the best deals for broadband. Remember, "broadband" is just a word used to describe any kind of fast Internet connection. You simply can't work cost-effectively without broadband these days; even entry-level packages are better value than the old dial-up alternative. Look into what types of broadband Internet are available in your area—big cities always have faster connections than rural areas.

When considering broadband, the most important factor is speed. How fast is the connection? Is it fast enough to do all the things you would like to be able to do? Internet transfer speeds are measured in kilobytes (KB) and megabytes (MB) per second. Here's a table to make it simple:

Even an entry-level 512KB broadband Internet connection is around 10 times faster than a standard 56KB dial-up Internet connection, allowing you to view web pages with almost no noticeable delay, and with an 8MB broadband connection you could watch TV-quality video through your computer. Here is a summary of what is on offer:

> **Best All-Rounder –** For the majority of Internet users, a 4MB deal will offer the best balance between price and performance.

> **Basic Dial-Up –** 256KB or 512KB doesn't offer the performance you'll need to be able to get the best out of streaming audio and video.

> **Fast connection –** 8MB and above is best for serious design studio work, sharing the Internet connection between two or more computers, downloading photographic files, or even playing a lot of games. A connection at the higher end of the scale (8MB upward) will allow you to take advantage of video and music on demand or broadband Internet and digital TV.

TIP

Be careful downloading free software, but remember there is plenty of good "free" shareware out there. If in any doubt, join a forum and post some questions; someone will have an answer for you.

www.designerstalk.com
www.graphicdesignforum.com
www.forums.adobe.com/index.jspa

TIP

The best money-saving tip regarding design software is to buy only the programs you really need and keep them up to date. Missing too many upgrades may render a program obsolete: buy version 3 of a program, miss a couple of free online upgrades, and before you know it, version 5 has been released and the company only sells upgrades from 4 to 5 because the upgrade from 3 to 5 has been deleted.

Internet connection speed	Time to load a typical web page (based on 100KB of data)	Time to load a typical 5-minute song (based on a 5MB MP3 file)	Streaming video quality
56KB dial-up modem	14secs	12mins 30sec	
256KB broadband	3secs	3mins	Low quality
512KB broadband	1.6secs	1min 30secs	
1MB broadband	0.8sec	41secs	
2MB broadband	0.4sec	20secs	Medium quality
4MB broadband	0.1sec	5secs	
6MB broadband	instant	instant	
8$^+$MB broadband	instant	instant	TV quality

> Images sourced online from iStockphoto, the Internet's original member-generated image and design community.

Communication between designer and client is essential. Often the best way to do this is to bypass the telephone and use e-mail. By avoiding costly phone rates, it is a great way to save money. Use e-mail to send attached PDF files to show clients your visuals; this saves even more money on paper outputs and couriers.

For files that are too big to e-mail, try one of the free online transfer sites (such as www.yousendit.com or www.getdropbox.com). These web-based digital content delivery services let users send, receive, and track files on demand. They provide an alternative to sending large e-mail attachments; using FTP sites; or sending CDs, DVDs, or USB flash drives through the post or via costly couriers. Sending under 100MB of information is free; larger files may require a paid account.

So, once you have your computer and have installed all your software, downloaded your chosen free fonts and activated your free system fonts, attached your printer, installed your Internet connection, and have your mouse at the ready, all you need is paying clients!

TIP

Avoid any deal with a monthly allowance of 1 gigabyte (GB) or less. Many deals offer a 15GB monthly allowance, but if you shop around you may be able to find a deal with an unlimited allowance for the same price. If you think you are likely to want to download large numbers of files, or you are a serious online gamer, go for a larger download limit, or better still, a deal with no limit.

TIP

Another important factor in your choice of broadband Internet deal is whether there is a download limit, often called a "usage allowance," and how high this limit is.

TIP

Use e-mail as a way of chatting to your clients and you will have created a permanent record of all that you have discussed and been asked to do. Always insist on using e-mail when asking a client to approve a job, especially if it's going to print, as it sets the date and time that approval was given. Never go to print on verbal consent alone.

TIP

How up to date is your computer? If it is less than five years old, there is probably nothing to worry about, but you should check that it meets any minimum requirements specified by the provider. If your computer is older, it may be unsuitable for broadband connection. If in doubt, the supplier should be able to offer advice.

CHAPTER 1: PLANNING

STAYNICE
THE NETHERLANDS

INVEST IN FUTURE WORK

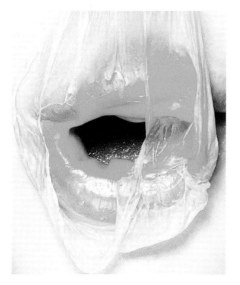

Finding the right clients to work with is every designer's dream; realistically, most designers won't get to pick and choose who they work with.

Business is business, and you need to put in place cost-saving parameters to keep your systems of finding the right clients efficient. Will it work to spend money on advertising yourself? Is it cost-effective to do mail drops or post out thousands of company brochures? For most creative agencies, the best way to win new clients is the cheapest—word of mouth. Get your clients to speak highly of you and recommend you to others, and you have a form of self-promotion and marketing that money simply cannot buy.

All clients seek value for money and an end product that will help create the image they want or that will make their product fly off the shelf. If this can be achieved and the designer has clearly made an effort to reduce overall spending, the greater the trust between client and designer will become. Once this trust has been established, the client may leave the designer the space they need to develop the brand and solve every new brief in a cost-effective manner. It is important that the designer also save money by not wasting time.

Only experience will tell you if a phone call is genuine or not and whether it's a pitch worth going for, but the following questions can be a good guide. How did they find you? It's good if you were recommended to them, not so good if they simply found you by chance. Are you one of many they are going to speak to? Are they simply building a tender list because it is company policy to get a certain number of quotes? If so, there is no guarantee they haven't already decided who to give the work to; they just need to get costs in from others anyway. Are they asking to see visuals along with quotes, but don't seem interested in meeting you or seeing any of your past work?

OH YEAH STUDIO
NORWAY

Norway's Oh Yeah Studio created this website for photographer Thomas Brun. Rather than receive payment for the work, the studio happily agreed to swap services, and used Brun's skills with the camera as payment.

Weigh up the pros and cons of a job. Realistically, what are the chances of getting this work? The more you are able to cut down on your own time being wasted, the more you are able to give time to genuine clients and charge them less. Save money by picking your projects wisely. Very rarely will a huge piece of work come from an e-mail that begins simply "Hi" and shows no attempt to actually make personal contact. If the first thing mentioned is a limited budget, try to find out how much this is up front and make sure you discuss what this budget has to allow for. Is it just for design time, or will it also need to cover copywriting, photography, illustration, and, more importantly, print? The best test for identifying whether a potential new client is seriously looking to commission design work is to ask them to meet with you. Going to someone's office is an excellent way to check they are genuine. If they come to you this is also a good sign that they are serious about the work. Many designers believe it is best not to supply a visual pitch or tender to anyone they have not met or spoken to. Insist on being able to present the tender and costs in person.

Once you have found your clients and agreed to work with them, and you know the parameters of their budgets and what they expect in return, only then can trust start to build and the fun begin.

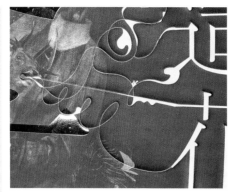

TIP

Remember, from the moment a client calls, try to find out if you are being asked to tender for this work against other agencies. This way you know from the start that the work is not guaranteed to come to you. Quite often you will be asked to submit visuals along with costs, without being informed that several other companies have also been invited to do so.

FLÁVIO HOBO
PORTUGAL

∧ This illustration is part of a calendar produced
› for Brazilian print house Idealiza. All the creatives who participated in the project provided their input free to ensure the project's survival and to see their work produced directly by the print house to the highest possible standards.

UNDERSTAND THE JOB AHEAD

▾ staynice's client offered a great spot to work—a former hotel in the seaside city of Vlissingen. The budget only covered some expenses, plus food and drinks, but the offer was too good to refuse. The studio opted to paint the surface by hand, using tape, brushes, and latex wall paint.

Early measures can be taken, right at the beginning of a project, to help keep costs down.

Whether you're working with a new client or an existing client, try to get them to come to you to discuss the new project. Explain that within your creative environment there is more visual material at hand to show them—from examples in design books or on the Internet, to samples of design from your own portfolio. You will save money on travel, but more importantly, you will save time by not leaving the studio. A client coming to you also shows that they are keen for the work to commence and that they believe you are worth taking the time to visit.

Make sure you use this time wisely. As obvious as this seems, you can save on costs by not having to have a second meeting simply because not enough was discussed at the first. A brief doesn't have to be typed, but take notes, ask lots of questions, know exactly what is being asked of you, and what the client wishes to achieve. Ask what they like and dislike, find out who their competitors are and why their products are selling better. Ask all of this and money will be saved by going down the right route to begin with. Communicate clearly with the client. They must be left in no doubt about what you are doing for them, the timescales involved, and the budgets available.

STAYNICE
THE NETHERLANDS

Lead the client. If you have a good idea, tell them. Be confident; after all, it's their money you are spending—they have to trust you. If you can save them money they will thank you for it. Take the initiative and show them what you have in mind. Explain the money-saving ideas you have and how you plan to realize them. Confirm and know for a fact that your production costs will actually cover everything promised. Don't lose your design fees by having to prop up spiraling production fees. If possible always allow for a small markup on production in case your supplier increases the cost or you forgot to add on delivery fees.

Consider and outline to the client all the things they can do themselves to save on further external costs before the design even begins. Can the client do their own copywriting? After all, surely they know about their business better than anyone else? This may actually speed up the whole process, saving time and money. Will the client be supplying the photography? If so, is it high enough resolution or good enough quality? Later in this book we will explore in more depth how to save money when buying imagery and creating your own illustration, and we will also look into economical ways of printing or supplying the final product.

MOODLEY
AUSTRIA

^ Instead of a large outdoor campaign to
< promote the upcoming plays of the Graz
Theater, Moodley's signs were made of
polystyrene in the form of an arrow. Instead
of spending large amounts on producing
and booking billboards, the relatively cheap
polystyrene arrows were placed in various
locations around the city where people least
expected to see them.

GET YOUR QUOTES CONFIRMED

...we're rela[x]

...rifare la camera

SUBTITLE
ITALY

✋ 🗇 ✍ 🗇

⌃ To maximize their budget for the Aquadulci Hotel in Sardinia, Subtitle used color sparingly, yet creatively. One, two, and four colors were used in combination with an uncoated stock.

It is vital that you organize budgets before you start any design work. You must get solid production costs in writing, whether print or digital, and set for a reasonable length of time.

If, for example, the cost of paper rises between your getting your quote and commissioning the print, and the printer will not honor their original quote, you may well have to make up the difference from your personal fees—the client may not be willing to discuss securing extra funding. Get at least three quotes, but think carefully about going with the cheapest printer. Can they supply as high a quality finish as the others? Why is it cheaper? Is the cost less because they have forgotten to add on the cost of delivery or the cost of finishing? If you have any doubts, pick up the phone or e-mail and get confirmation that the quote is accurate. Never trust a supplier, print or otherwise, to honor a quote they have supplied to you should something go wrong. Always check it carefully.

To get the most accurate quote, be as clear as possible about what you're actually asking for. Vague or unclear print quote requests tend to produce inaccurate estimates, which may become more costly when you deliver the final artwork to the supplier. Always tell your supplier how many you need, but get a second cost for an increased run to get a comparison. For example, if you only want 1,000 of an item, also ask what 2,000 would cost.

If you are getting a quote from an illustrator, photographer, or any other creative, it's very important you agree on who owns the copyright in the work. If your client requests a reprint six months later, will you have to get repeat permission from the photographer or illustrator, and will you have to pay them royalties?

TIP

A good way to get an accurate quote is to use a supplier quote form. This will lead you through the various questions that need to be answered. Most good printing companies will provide such a form on their website (as well as the facility to upload final artwork), or can e-mail or fax one to you.

TIP

Run-ons in printing are often inexpensive. Once initial print costs have been worked out, the only difference is the amount of paper and any finishing and/or delivery involved. If the client asks for 800 brochures, also give them a cost for 1,000. There is usually very little difference in cost to round up the quantity.

Carefully consider what type of stock you require. Stock (or paper) is critical to the pricing of your work. If you're producing a brochure, consider whether the cover will be on a different material from the inside pages. Money can be saved by producing a "self cover." This is good for smaller documents of 16 pages or less, as it involves a single weight of paper throughout the brochure. And remember, you must stick to multiples of four pages unless you want to end up with expensive foldouts. Most standard brochures are made up of flat sheets that are twice the finished size of the final document. These pages print both sides of the paper and are then folded and stapled to the other pages. It is this printing of both sides and folding that creates a four-page set. For example, a 16-page brochure is made up of four larger sheets printed both sides, then folded and stapled together. Adding another sheet would make it 20 pages, and so on. If this weren't done, the staples or binding would have nothing to grip and the pages would simply fall out. If a job requires an extra two pages only, this has to be built in as a foldout. This means that, technically, instead of an additional four-page section, a six-page section is needed, and this requires a much bigger sheet size, which adds to the overall cost.

Finally, remember that the difference between good design and bad is usually a well thought-through solution. You can't cover up bad design with expensive print.

TIP

People often think that glossy paper is expensive. In reality it is no more pricey than most other papers, from a silk to a matte.

> A reputable design company will honor its quotes and not increase them without good reason. It is vital that these are as accurate as possible and cover all the required elements of a client's job. If you forget to include a cost and the client has approved your prices, it may be very difficult to go back and ask for more.

CHAPTER 2: DESIGN PROCESS

JOSHUA GAJOWNIK
USA

STAY ON BUDGET

Nothing is more important than staying on budget. If a cost has been agreed with the client, it can be very difficult to go and ask for more, even if it is not your fault.

Look at all the factors and decide if it's worth risking asking the client to increase their funds. Will they use you again if you are seen to increase your costs over those originally quoted? If the client asks for something not originally quoted for or increases the size of the document, then you have every right to propose increasing the budget. If the cost of paper or printing increases before you get approval from your client, you may not feel you can ask them to make up the shortfall. Unless more than three months has passed since you were quoted on a job, it is advisable to simply refuse to pay the increase proposed by your supplier. Explain that the increase will damage your relationship with your client and suggest that you will take your work to another printer/manufacturer if they do not honor their initial costs. Always remember to be fair. Arguing with a supplier and not giving them anywhere to go in a debate will only result in them saying no. If this does happen, you may simply have to re-tender the project and bring in another printer or manufacturer. Do everything you can to avoid your client getting involved in or even knowing about the potential cost problem; just solve it for them—this is part of your job.

> The aim of NoChintz's stationery is to be vivid, strong, flexible, and eco-friendly. The use of one consistent color reinforces the brand and allows easy replication using items like fluoro tape and labels. Using recycled stocks, and branding items with stickers saves money, yet has a big impact.

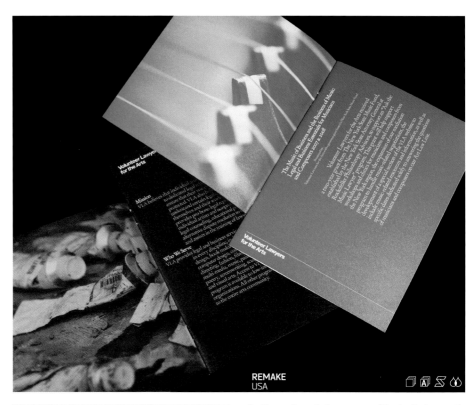

REMAKE
USA

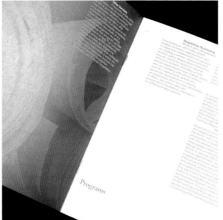

^ Two-color printing was used for budgetary and
‹ conceptual reasons: the pairs of related colors used on each piece represent the two voices (artist and lawyer) engaged in the dialog offered by Volunteer Lawyers for the Arts (VLA). The budget also necessitated the least expensive stock photography, which was then treated in order to form a more cohesive visual language for VLA. Innovative print and binding techniques (overprinting metallic inks on other colors to create an illusion of depth and cutting covers short to reveal the page underneath) contributed to the interest created by each piece. Printed by Riegelmann Printing in New York.

NO CHINTZ
UK

Take heart from that fact that most clients simply want the very best design work they can get for their brand, but it is not in their best interest to waste lots of time rejecting work. Most designers have excellent relationships with their clients and this builds trust, which, in return, will save time and money.

If you have the client's trust, you can start implementing good saving structures, which, in turn, will make you more profit for your design time and, just as importantly, allow you to bill your client lower overall fees as the work goes smoothly from start to finish. This is the ideal situation for both designer and client. With this trust in place you can keep costs down by sending visuals and proofs electronically, by e-mail, PDF, or web download, etc.

Try to use your time wisely. A meeting with the client to take the initial brief, and presenting the first visuals face-to-face always works well. Alterations, design tweaks, and new visuals generally do not need face-to-face meetings. Keep track of your time, both in and out of the studio. If you monitor how long a job takes, you will be able to see where time can be saved for future projects. It's not always necessary to keep daily time sheets, but a good studio manager or director will know how long should be allocated to a project and can increase or decrease this time as required. No two jobs are identical, but they can often be similar. Learn from each job you do and you will soon learn to work more efficiently, which, in return, will allow for lower bills, but higher profits.

If a client changes the brief, increases the amount of copy and therefore the number of pages needed, or ups the quantity of the finished product they require, then you must get a new quote to them, in writing, immediately, and be sure to receive written notification that these costs have been accepted and you are to continue. E-mail is great for this as it is fast and as good as a written letter. Never accept permission verbally or trust that they will simply pay the invoice when you present it. You are a supplier and if things go wrong you will have to be able to prove that you were working under instruction and that the client has broken their contract with you. And that is not easy.

A gray area is if the client simply doesn't like the work you have presented and you have spent a lot of time on it. This is difficult as they may claim you failed to supply goods as proposed and to the standard expected. This happens to all of us at some point. What you might think is fantastic design, your client may feel is too arty or simply not the right tone to represent their brand. Remember, they hold all the strings and will not pay you unless they are happy to do so. If a client rejects job after job, you will be losing design time and money. Ask yourself if you are the right designer for them and whether they are the sort of client you want to work with. Sometimes you simply have to walk away and admit defeat.

ONE SPOT COLOR

Up Projects commissioned REG to produce a series of marketing materials, postcards, and invites for The Other Flower Show. Not only was printing in single spot colors cheaper than full color, it also raised the production quality. Spot inks give a far more vibrant color than conventional full color.

REG
UK

Choosing to design in one spot color will reduce the cost implications of printing or producing a document, but the design will have to work much harder to get its message across. In some ways the design will really have to lend itself to printing in a spot color to work properly.

Color, and the way we use it, can add real impact to a design. Restricting yourself to just the one can be quite a challenge. How do you create an interesting design and vary the image and message when all you have is a single color? It's not easy, but when it's done right it gives brilliant and powerful results.

Single-color printing is the easiest form of production for the printing industry and this is why it's significantly cheaper.

One-color printing often uses the standard black ink on white paper, but varying the ink to one of the 1,100-plus unique, numbered inks of the PANTONE Solid color collection is an option and can create a different and eye-catching look. Another option would be to vary ink color and paper color to create an even more dramatic look. And remember, you can also use tints of the single spot color to vary the levels of intensity of your print.

FABRICE PRAEGER
FRANCE

GIVE UP ART
UK

Where process printing creates colors by combining the four process colors of cyan, magenta, yellow, and black (CMYK), four plates are needed, one for each color. Spot colors, otherwise known as PANTONE Matching System (PMS) colors, are each a single ink formulation. Because only one plate is needed for the spot color and tints of that color, it is usually more economical to print a spot-color job. Should you wish to add black or any other color, printing would require an additional plate, one for each color.

‹ Tempa records wanted to release a series of limited-edition, colored vinyl singles. To keep within budget, the outer sleeves were designed to be identical and produced with one spot color in one large print run, for use as required with each release. Specially placed die-cuts allow portions of the vinyl to show through, for differentiation between each release. The exposed areas of vinyl are such that the playable area of the discs will not get damaged. The labels were also printed in one color only, to match the vinyl as closely as possible.

Spot color showing
Pantone® Red 032C and tints

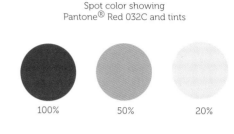

100%   50%   20%

❯ The cost-cutting technique with this CD cover was very simple: the use of just one spot color—black.

FLÁVIO HOBO
PORTUGAL

‹ This invitation for French and German television channel Arte, which folds out to a poster, was printed in a single spot color with a real fingerprint added by hand and in various colors, making each one unique and cost-effective.

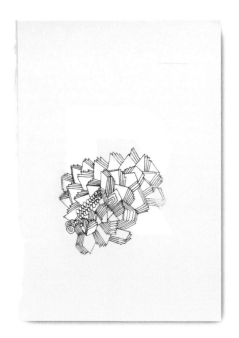

^ We are Public designed a series of prints to promote the Urban Art Show. "Perhaps the best part of the identity, and easily the most cost-effective, was the issuing of single-color interactive cards the week before the show," states Nicholas Jeeves.

WE ARE PUBLIC
UK

‹ Blok created this stationery for Mexican company Taller de Empresa. "We sometimes forget the power a one-color job beautifully produced may have."

TIP

Don't rely on the colors you see on-screen unless you have a color-calibrated monitor. Your screen uses a different system for displaying colors (RGB) to that used for printing (CMYK).

TIP

Use spot colors creatively. With careful combinations of the solid color and tints, and careful consideration of layout and typography, designs can have a massive impact without the expense of full-color process printing.

BLOK
BRAZIL

CASE STUDY:
PURPOSE

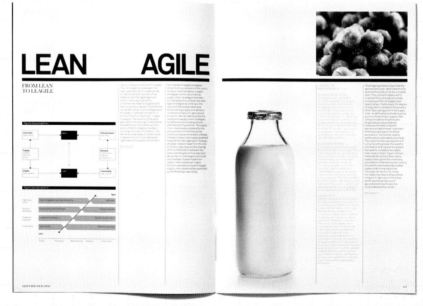

Purpose created *View* magazine for clients EFFP. It is printed in a single spot color throughout.

Designers Stuart Youngs, Paul Felton, and Adam Browne wanted to create a magazine that was typographically based. This reduced the costs of commissioning photography or illustration and, in return, allowed them to experiment with type, solids, and white space. The result is a stunning collection of spreads that didn't require a massive budget. Savings were used to print onto Think4 from Howard Smith Paper. Printing sets two-up on a B2 (707 × 500mm/27⁵/₁₆ × 19¹¹/₁₆in) sheet reduced production fees further by minimizing waste. All of the images and illustrations used were sourced from low-cost stock websites.

SHADRACH LINDO
USA

^ Monotone images beautifully produced using a single spot black. These full-color images were converted to grayscale in Photoshop and brought together as one large montage.

TIP

No access to a PANTONE swatch book or PANTONE software to specify a specific color? Create your design using solid black (and tints of black), and give your artwork to the printer along with a sample of something in a very similar color to what you would like your job printed in. The printers will be able to use their swatch books to get a very close match. All reputable printers will be happy to do this for you without charge as it is in their interest not only to get the work, but also to know exactly what colors they are to print.

TIP

Experiment with spot colors on different-colored paper stocks and take note of how this varies the final appearance of the design.

> This design uses a single spot black alongside blind embossing to create a minimalist, but visually powerful business card.

THREEWHITE
JAPAN

ART DIRECTION AN

t director: 田中 美帆

A fantastic range of stationery created by B&W Studio for professional photographer Barry Milliken. Printed in a single spot color (black), the letterheads, comp. slips, and business cards all come together to spell out the photographer's name.

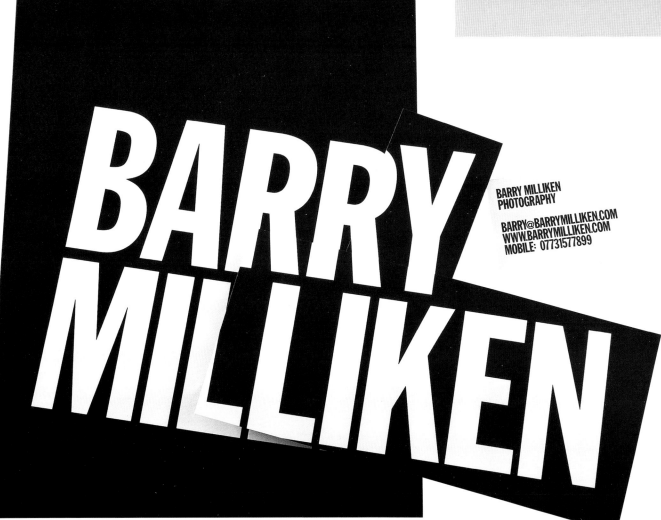

BARRY MILLIKEN
PHOTOGRAPHY

BARRY@BARRYMILLIKEN.COM
WWW.BARRYMILLIKEN.COM
MOBILE: 07731577899

B&W STUDIO
UK

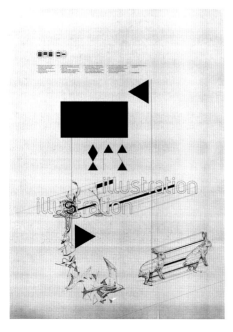

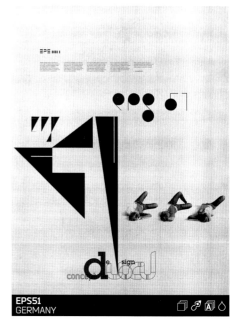

▲ A series of posters by Berlin-based eps51 for *Brownbook* magazine, Dubai. The designers wanted to show that big budgets and glossy effects are not always equivalent to high-quality workmanship. In this case the low budget was concept rather than necessity. To create a contrast to Dubai's artificial and glossy cityscape and architecture, eps51 kept all graphics black-and-white and printed using a cheap black-and-white digital printer onto 100gsm paper.

▶ Design Report for the Salone Internazionale del Mobile in Milan by Projekttriangle. This was created to a very small production budget as the client is a nonprofit organization. Using end-of-line papers, the designers created a generic design that could be used throughout the project, and printed it using only a single spot color.

TIP

To create a "ghost" image of your text or logo in the background of your work, change its values to 10% of the full-color strength.

With no full-color printing, these invitations, for client Centrum Beeldemde, took their inspiration from grafitti tags. A spot silver ink was printed onto 350gsm papers of various colors.

DC WORKS
THE NETHERLANDS

The Northern Clay Center, an arts center dedicated to the enhancement of ceramic arts, commissioned this exhibition brochure. Veto chose to print a single spot, opaque white directly onto colored offset card.

VETO DESIGN
USA

> Bangkok-based Akarit Leeyavanich, at Default Design, created this stunning range of packaging for skin and aesthetic center Face2Face, in Phuket. Printing each label in a single spot color reduces the overall cost, but most importantly creates a simple, easily recognizable product with its own color-coordinating system to distinguish one piece of packaging in the range from the next.

DEFAULT DESIGN
THAILAND

˅ To keep costs down, this logo was designed as a one-color (black only) mark, with limited color applications that were printed digitally; or in screens of black, for single-color printing. Promotional materials and newsletters were printed in-house on black and color laser printers, or saved as downloadable PDF files. All letterheads, envelopes, and business cards were printed digitally. Using only black also worked from a stylistic standpoint: Tenth Church wanted an identity that was bold, simple, and contemporary.

NANCY WU ART & DESIGN
CANADA

^ The brief for Studio Astrid Stavro was to produce
< promotional literature explaining the Art Directors
Club of Europe and their awards program. It had
to be inexpensive to produce and manageable
to post. An A2 poster was produced that cross-
folded down to standard envelope size. Each side
printed a single spot color and could be used
independently of the other side.

> This brochure was created to promote
Moonlight, an outdoor cinema, to potential
advertisers and sponsors. Creating on an
extremely tight budget, the designers added
impact by printing a picnic-blanket pattern
in a single spot color, and used this to
wrap the actual brochure prior to sending
it out. The front cover image was shot by
the designers and a standard yellow
self-adhesive sticker, printed in a single
spot color, was used to seal the package.

NAUGHTYFISH
AUSTRALIA

TWO SPOT COLORS

▼ Designed by DC Works, this booklet was to assist the promotion of creative festivals within the Rotterdam area. By using two spot colors throughout the entire brochure, enough money was saved to fund additional mock backstage bracelets placed within the booklet.

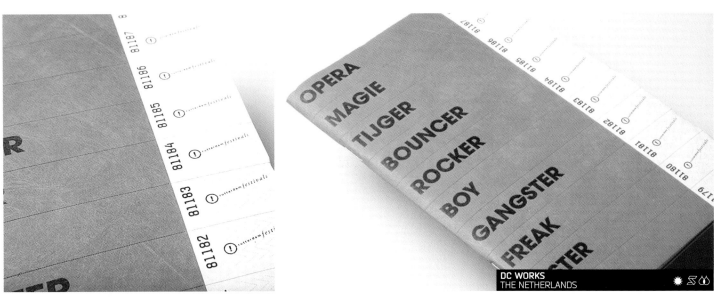

DC WORKS
THE NETHERLANDS

The jump from one-color to two-color printing brings with it a myriad of possibilities and opportunities for the designer.

Two-color printing commonly uses black and one other color to give your artwork a more dramatic feel, but you can also use two spot colors, and with over 1,000 spot colors from which to choose, there is a huge range of options available. Select two colors that will work in harmony; avoid clashing colors unless you are using this to make a deliberate statement.

Try combining your two spot colors along with their tints for even more color possibilities.

Reversing text out of spot colors can give typography a true stand-out effect. Use solid colors or a dark tint to provide the best contrast.

Another good effect is to overprint your text onto solid areas of your secondary spot color. To get the best contrast, use a light spot color alongside a dark spot color, or two strongly contrasting colors from the same range—a light cyan on top of a rich dark blue can look fantastic.

To push things even further, explore the unique results achievable with spot colors by choosing a metallic ink or other special type of ink. Mixing spot colors with metallic colors can create truly distinctive effects, especially if these are overprinted direct and not knocked through the secondary color.

‹ Created by Brazilian design house Blok for a low-income technical school located in an impoverished area of Mexico City, this diary was created to reflect the proud, bold, and positive outlook adopted by the school. Printed on low-cost paper as a two-spot-color job, the bright neon yellow created a bold, bright, and standout piece of design.

❤ Music's poster for the short film *No Way Through*. The film itself highlights mobility and movement restrictions imposed by governments around the world, especially those in war zones. The poster graphically represents the film's topic in the form of a maze. Music designed the maze so that, if you follow its path with a pen, you end up creating the title of the film. Simply printed in two spot colors, it creates a powerful graphic reminiscent of the film's content.

BLOK
BRAZIL

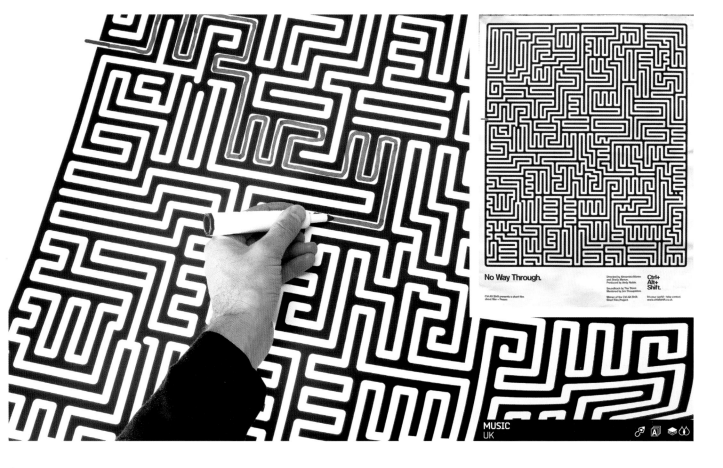

No Way Through.

MUSIC
UK

CASE STUDY:
REMAKE

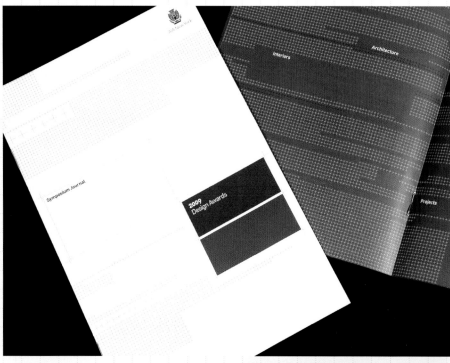

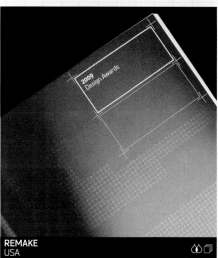

REMAKE
USA

Remake's Michael Dyer explains how two colors enabled him to produce great design work which came in not just on, but below budget.

"The Design Awards and Building Type Awards Program is an annual competition held by the AIGA's New York chapter. It comprises a host of printed material and an exhibition, all of which had to be produced within tight budget constraints.

"For this reason, two-color printing was used throughout, with process magenta representing the Design Awards, and gray the Building Type Awards.

"All paper was the printer's house stock (reducing costs further) and was run on as few forms as possible to maximize efficiency. Some pieces were designed backwards from the allowable space on the form.

"For the exhibition, a series of wall-mounted panels formed the core of the design system. The exhibition's visual language was routered out of the panels and became a flexible positioning system for project boards, which were simple inkjet prints mounted onto foamcore. This allowed the project cost to come in significantly under budget."

DUOTONES FROM TWO SPOT COLORS

Duotone images are created by starting with a grayscale image and reproducing it using tonal values of two different spot colors. A light blue and a dark blue can work together to create a fantastic duotone that seems to reflect a range of blues; two opposite colors, such as red and green, can create a striking, almost posterized graphic image. Printing images using the duotone method produces a richer, longer tone scale than is possible using the restrictive range of only one spot color.

Creating a duotone is best done in Adobe Photoshop by converting the image from CMYK to grayscale, then to duotone, and using the duotone curves to develop the strengths that each spot will have within the image.

TIP

Printing with two spot colors often costs only a fraction more than printing with a single spot color. Most printers will have a small two-color printing press tucked away in the corner of the factory in order to avoid down-time on the full-color press by using it for a two-color print. While a single spot color only uses one of the two rollers on a two-color press, you will be paying for your time on that machine anyway; bringing a second spot color, and hence the second roller, into the frame is the most economical use of the printing press.

SCALE TO FIT
THE NETHERLANDS

‹ Scale to Fit were restricted by a limited budget
∧ when commissioned by BNN to create a brand book focusing on a broadcaster's ability to be constantly fluid. The concept of a "DIY activity book" included marker pens. The book is printed in two colors and is numbered by hand, with full-color pictures and stickers (printed on a separate sheet) individually glued in place, making each copy unique.

‹ BUROPONY were invited to design an album cover for Chega Recordings for a track called "Nocha Dura" which translates as "All Night." The two spot colors used to create the artwork add to the raw feel when combined with the lo-res web pics cut-and-pasted together.

STUDIO EMMI
UK

❤ This book for teachers helps to introduce music into a school's curriculum. The whole book was printed in two colors. The cover is constructed as eight pages and is cut shorter and narrower than the inner pages. For longevity, the wire hook binding allows the book to be stored in teachers' folders, together with any printouts/tests/papers for each individual class. (Illustrations by Emily Alston.)

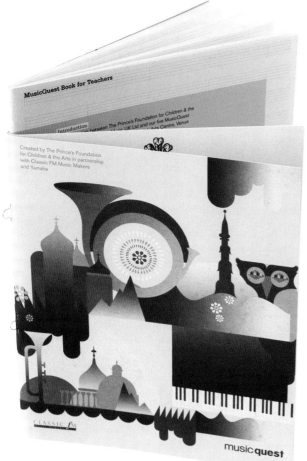

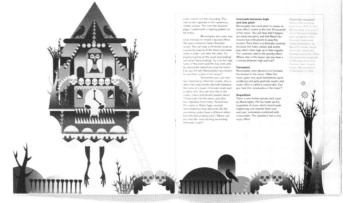

CHRISTOF NARDIN
AUSTRIA

❧ This two-spot-color poster, using metallic spot gold and black, was created for a series of lectures at the University of Applied Arts Vienna. Using a metallic spot color alongside a regular spot color can create very striking and memorable graphics. The static spot color stays constant while light reflects and changes the tones and visibility of the underlying metallic color.

University of Applied Arts Vienna presents an interdisciplinary lecture series organized by the department of Design History & Theory with the departments of Graphic Design and Fashion

MON 05/12/05, 7PM
Joanne Entwistle (UK), Fashion Theory

TUE 13/12/05, 7PM
åbäke (UK), Graphic Design

TUE 10/01/06, 7PM
Erik Kessels (NL)
Advertising & Communication

TUE 17/01/06, 7PM
Penny Martin (UK)
Fashion Theory & Publishing

MON 23/01/06, 7PM
Anuschka Blommers, Niels Schumm (NL)
Photographers

diː'ʌŋgewʌndtə
University of Applied Arts Vienna
Oskar Kokoschka-Platz 2, A-1010 Vienna
www.uni-ak.ac.at/cuts

❧ This poster is beautifully illustrated and printed with two spot colors.

ANDY SMITH
UK

An excellent example of design using two spot colors combined with strong typography and layout. The simplicity, color, and layout of these business cards ensure that they will not be forgotten or missed.

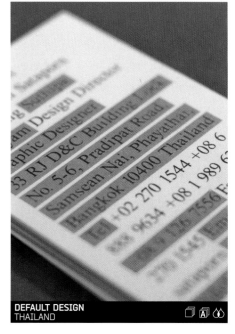

DEFAULT DESIGN
THAILAND

This event literature was cross-folded and printed with two spot colors on both sides.

HEYDUK, MUSIL & STRNAD
CZECH REPUBLIC

TIP

Restricting yourself to two spot colors will reduce the overall costs. Generally speaking, if you use more than two spot colors, it may be more economical to simply print using four-color process (CMYK) litho-printing, though the colors may not be so vibrant. Talk to your printer for the most cost-effective approach.

CASE STUDY:
ADHEMAS BATISTA

ADHEMAS BATISTA
BRAZIL

The Grateful Palate is a unique food brand with creative and tasteful products aimed at the US and Australian markets.

With an enormous and very creative wine portfolio including brands such as Evil, Bitch, and Roogle (a creature half eagle, half kangaroo), The Grateful Palate [www.gratefulpalate.com] commissioned designer and illustrator Adhemas Batista to create a new identity and design everything from the bottle caps to the boxes, labels, logotypes, names, and characters. Batista worked with spot colors to create a fascinating and immensely strong series of designs which ensure that the product has maximum shelf presence.

CASE STUDY:
WE ARE PUBLIC

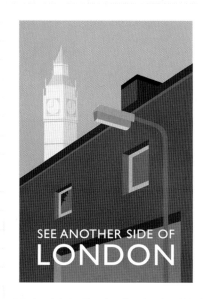

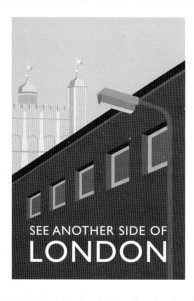

Design consultancy We are Public have embraced the technique of spot-color printing with exemplary results

The Capital Community Foundation (dedicated to funding community-based action that improves the lives of London's most disadvantaged) works hard to stay in touch with its donor list and to recruit new members to its excellent cause. This set of postcards (shown on the left) encourages recipients to see a different side of London from the one popularly expressed by tourist guides. It uses tints of black and single spot colors throughout. Postcards were released at three-month intervals to create a year of regular correspondence at minimal cost.

The Capital Community Foundation Annual Report 08–09 (shown right) was designed to spark new ways of delivering and extending the client's message while keeping the spend at a minimum. The Foundation's two-color rebrand was completed a few months before the report (both the work of art director Nicholas Jeeves). The strong red-and-black palette inspired an illustration-led approach, with London's ubiquitous pigeons as a vocal supporting act. Further expense was saved with a small print run in stage one, followed by PDF delivery later in the year.

WE ARE PUBLIC
UK

WE WORK
WITH THOSE AT
THE GRASSROOTS

WE WORK
WITH LONDON
BOROUGHS

"WHEN I FIRST SAW
'THE WIZARD OF OZ' IT MADE
A WRITER OUT OF ME."

SALMAN RUSHDIE

Foreword

From the Chairs of BFI, Film Club,
Film Education, First Light Movies,
UK Film Council and Skillset

Introduction

Film inspires, excites, informs and moves. It has often been
described as the great art form of the twentieth century;
and it has certainly been one of the most popular.

WE LIVE IN AN AGE WHEN TO BE
LITERATE MEANS TO BE AS FAMILIAR
WITH IMAGES ON A SCREEN AS WITH
TEXT ON A PAGE, AND TO BE AS
CONFIDENT WITH A CAMERA OR A
KEYBOARD AS WITH A PEN.

WE ARE PUBLIC
UK

> Designed by Brazilian agency ps.2 arquitetura +
> design, these monthly programs are for the
visual arts and new media courses offered by
SESC Pompéia. They were designed to be
editable by the client for future editions and
thus keep costs down. Instead of photography,
the design uses a base grid of circles. It is
printed on cheap uncoated paper, always in
two spot colors only.

PS.2 ARQUITETURA + DESIGN
BRAZIL

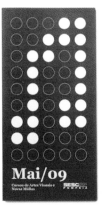

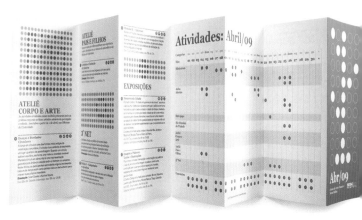

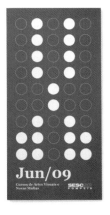

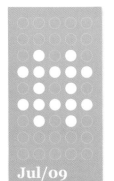

GRAPHISTERIE GÉNÉRALE
LUXEMBOURG

> A packaging series with each range
> individually produced in two spot colors.

CASE STUDY:
JOSHUA GAJOWNIK

Windhover is North Carolina State University's award-winning literary and artistic annual.

Created by US designer Joshua Gajownik, these annuals are a tour de force of spot-color design and print. Gajownik recalls, "Budgets were tight and heavily scrutinized. Once designs were accepted, the work was curated to maximize print efficiency. Avoiding full-color printing, the book begins and ends with two spot-color signature pages. The cost savings were significant. We even managed to save on restricted page sizes allowing more pages to be printed together on the one sheet. The savings were so significant that a little 'extra treat' was allowed in the form of a spot UV varnish on the cover, something we simply never thought we could afford."

JOSHUA GAJOWNIK
USA

FULL-COLOR PRINTING

Printing in full color (CMYK lithography) is the most common form of printing for large-run commercial work.

It is the most economic way to print a large number of posters, fliers, or brochures in which photographs are required to show a product or place and color is required to show these at their very best. There is no point trying to sell cars, sofas, or jackets through a black-and-white brochure when the first thing the consumer asks is "What does it look like in red?"

EDHV
THE NETHERLANDS

∧
‹ Pushing full-color print to its limits! A series of stunning images created for printers Greve Offset. Full-color print was produced and then reprinted on top of itself through a second run.

Full-color printing combines the four primary colors: cyan, magenta, yellow, and black. Together these can produce the full range of printable colors, with the exception of specialty colors such as metallics or foils. It can be used to match single spot colors, but it doesn't give the same solidity. If we needed to produce a CMYK match for Pantone Red 032 C, the breakdown, based on the Pantone swatch book values range, would be:

Cyan = 0%
Magenta = 92%
Yellow = 65%
Black = 0%

Remember, as a separate plate is produced for each of the four colors, this will add to the cost of print compared to printing single spot colors, which only need one plate per color.

VETO DESIGN
USA

∧ Perfectly printed full-color litho work on an uncoated stock. A sealer varnish was required to avoid ink rub-off onto the white text areas.

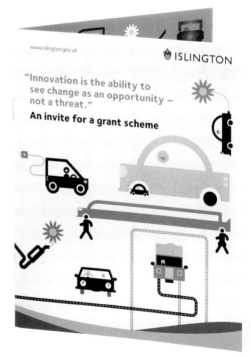

∧ The aim of this design was to create a brochure that business owners would find visually stimulating and easy to read. All inner text pages print in a single spot black, allowing the remaining budget to be spent on a full-color cover.

BEAM
UK

› Kuizin used full-color print with an additional fluorescent ink for this cover.

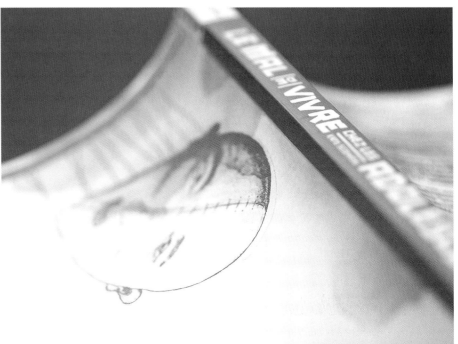

KUIZIN STUDIO
CANADA

Explore the unexpected
Walk Islington

ISLINGTON

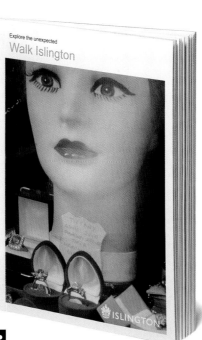

Explore the unexpected
Walk Islington

ISLINGTON

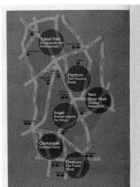

Fancy a walk?

It's the easiest way to get to know all those things you never knew about your local area – where to buy the best cheese in London, which house was home to a famous poet who lost their head at the church. This guide aims not only to whet your appetite for exploring Islington but also to remind you of the pleasures and benefits of simply walking more.

In all there are six walks around the borough – choose to discover the atmospheric graveyards and churches of historic Finsbury (p10), the famous markets, creative communities and impressive squares of Clerkenwell (p18), the green fields and dells of Highbury (p26), the abundance of playgrounds and restaurants in Tufnell Park (p34), the secret passages and boutique shops of Angel (p40) and the leafy nature of the New River Walk (p50). You'll see the many different sides of Islington from the best angle – on foot.

^ Beam split this brochure into three sections,
‹ printing the front and back on a cheap sugar paper in two spot colors, so that they could replace the magenta with a CMYK substitute to match the fluorescent pink Pantone special, and adjust the CMYK images accordingly.

BEAM
UK

SOCIO DESIGN
UK

^ Self-promotional, full-color work, finished with a spot UV varnish.

KVORNING DESIGN & KOMMUNIKATION
DENMARK

< For the Danish stand at the 2008 Womex World Music Expo, a poster and brochure were required to list the Danish exhibitors. To reduce printing costs and allow Kvorning to print in full color, the two were combined: when unfolded, the brochure took the form and look of a poster.

CMYK
DIGITAL

For a long time digital printing was avoided by designers at all costs. It looked cheap, colors were often washed out, and the finishing was appalling; there was no scoring prior to folding, the fit was poor, and the paper quality was awful.

Thankfully, those days are behind us. Find a good digital printer and you will be delighted with the results. Digital printing can be very cheap and very quick, as it does not require drying time.

This poster was produced to give seven separate leaflets and six small fliers from the one "parent" poster. Printed digitally from an online printing house, the posters were then split up into their constituent parts by a studio in Berlin that specialized in cutting and folding.

‹ With a very low budget and a production run
⌄ of only 200 each, Both Lettera22 and P. Soleri
CD production costs were reduced by digitally
printing a 7in, black-and-white sleeve onto
300gsm board, and handbuilding. Artiva Design
even applied the self-adhesive CD blocks by
hand, and the disks were digitally printed in
a single color on a small ink-jet printer.

ARTIVA DESIGN
ITALY

Digital printing does not require plates
and uses toner powder instead of liquid
inks. This means that it does not require
million-dollar Heidelberg printing presses—
it uses the much cheaper color copiers
from manufacturers such as OKI, Xerox,
and Hewlett-Packard. Over time, and with
the advance in technology, the quality of
print from these machines has improved
greatly. Although the results are still not
quite as good as standard full-color litho
printing, it would take a trained eye to
spot the difference.

Another big advantage in digital printing is
the ease with which data can be changed.
It is very easy to personalize a job so that
each piece has a different name or identity
number, which is excellent for invitations
or promotional mailings. Digital printers
at the top end of the scale can also
bind, collate, and staple a job to rival the
finishing offered by conventional printers.

ARTIVA DESIGN
ITALY

❮ Designed for a departing teacher, this book contains a number of stories
❮ by fellow teachers, in text and image, on his favorite topic—culture clash.
BUROPONY adopted this theme as the leading design concept, with a clash
in patterns, layout, and type. An almost extinct dot-matrix printer was used
to label all the books individually, which cut the costs of the cover; and
printing only two parts of the book in full-color digital kept the book's costs
to a minimum.

Digital printing is excellent for the "home"
designer producing small quantities of
unique pieces, from wedding stationery to
handmade company brochures targeting
specific people or agencies. Modern
digital printing has revolutionized the fast-
turnaround, low-quantity design market.

For print runs under 200, the cost and
speed of digital printing simply cannot
be beaten. However, for anything over a
few hundred, conventional litho printing
starts to look more cost-effective. It's quite
simple. Most digital printers will charge
you per print, so, if you only need 20
copies, the bill will be very low. If you
print 20 copies of a job by standard litho
printing, the costs will be astronomical
because of the initial setup costs.

BUROPONY
THE NETHERLANDS

❮ Although the outer covers were foil-blocked onto GF Smith Colorplan, Glasgow-based Traffic commissioned specialist printers 21Color to print all inner pages onto house Silk digitally, and use copper staples to stitch the pages. The result was a beautifully finished, short-run, full-color digital brochure promoting two luxury homes built by Burns Interior Design.

TRAFFIC DESIGN CONSULTANTS
UK

The other downside of digital printing is that it limits your paper choice. Because digital printing uses powder rather than ink, it cannot produce a good result on a heavily textured paper: the powder sits on top of the paper rather than soaking into it as an ink would. With textured papers, the liquid ink of litho printing gives a better depth of color. Weigh up the pros and cons of both styles of printing, but learn to love digital printing, and when to use it, and it's a sure way of dramatically cutting production costs and turnaround times.

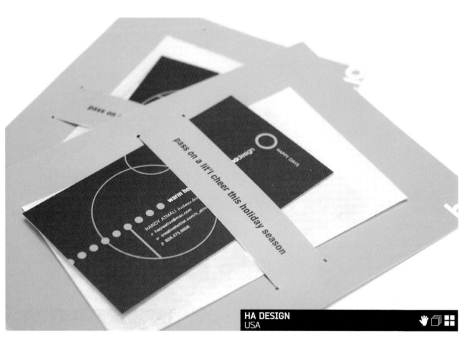

HA DESIGN
USA

❮ This self-promotional mailing converted digitally printed business cards into gift tags; with all the scoring and hole-punching completed by hand, costs were kept down.

CASE STUDY:
DESIGN BY IF

The Susans logo was created in Adobe Illustrator, but all other works were hand-drawn with pen on paper before being taken into Adobe Photoshop, Illustrator, and InDesign at various stages of the design process. All print was created using CMYK Digital.

Susans was a new company with a very limited budget. Space was also at a premium, so there was little room for boxes of stationery and packaging.

The logo shows three Yorkshire roses, which came to represent Susan and her two daughters, while the Scottish thistle refers to her late husband.

A blank space on the back of the card allows for a handwritten price so that, with a quick hole punch and a knotted thread, this eye-catching business card becomes a swing tag. Stickers provide a cheap, quick, and easy way to brand anything from stationery to sandwich packs.

A blog, with a simple header, was set up to provide a very cost-effective way to communicate Susans' potential to clients online. This avoided the often heavy costs associated with building a traditional website from scratch.

> This special Eskimo pack was given out to select prospects and clients, so just a small production run was required. All items in the pack were digitally printed onto board to reduce costs; the plastic elements had to be screenprinted.

HA DESIGN
USA

SOCIO DESIGN
UK

‹ HA Design used an online printer who offered a deal on free envelopes, which meant this successful mailing was produced with very little expense.

SCREEN-PRINTING

Screenprinting, an ancient and very basic art, is a valuable method of home printing, and a reasonably simple and affordable one at that.

Printing by this method is comparable to using stencils. The background design is painted onto a special, but inexpensive screen with printing paste, then dye is squeezed through the untreated areas of the screen. For each color required you need a separate screen, but from these screens many prints can then be produced.

Favored for its versatility, kitsch character, and unique color reproduction, screen-printing is a reliable method for producing work both efficiently and affordably. It serves the likes of students, illustrators, and pretty much anyone looking for an affordable and effective solution for producing limited-edition prints, printed clothing, non-paper-based printing, and promotional items, to name but a few.

‹ The press kit for performing artist Mama Lou was housed in a DVD case. The cases were screenprinted in one color on brown Kraft paper, which was also used for the envelopes. The kits were assembled by the client as required.

ANDY GABBERT
USA

MARK CANESO
USA

Screenprinting provides the massive benefit of allowing you to print onto absolutely anything—metal, plastic, paper, wood, fabric, or even concrete—which opens up huge avenues for the designer, and the client, to explore without having to worry about frightening costs for specialized printing. With screenprinting you can do all the printing by yourself—with a bit of practice, of course.

Makeshift screenprinting setups are something that many designers have in their home or studio in order to create small in-house editions. This gives them complete control of the piece from start to finish, with a quality every bit as good as the professionals. And you don't have to spend a fortune on the basic equipment in order to start screenprinting.

MATTHIAS DUNKEL
GERMANY

^ To keep the costs down for this poster for Otis College, Mark Caneso of pprwrk studio decided to screenprint the posters. Due to the low numbers needed, it was the most efficient way to create the desired effect. Caneso personally printed each poster with gold metallic ink on 100lb French Paper.

> Album design and promotional literature for the band The Rewind Life. All work produced, from CD to posters, was screenprinted in one color (black) on a homemade screenprinting table. The main booklet was copied in a local copy shop and hand-folded.

ANDY SMITH
UK

‹ Andy Smith has worked for brands including Nike, Mercedes, Orange, and Sony. He combines illustration and typography to create images with humor, energy, and optimism.

CASE STUDY:
LANDLAND

Landland is a small graphic design and illustration studio in Minneapolis, USA. It was founded by Dan Black, Jessica Seamans, and Matt Zaun in 2007.

Collectively Landland explains, "We had all been making things for quite a while, but 2007 was when we actually moved into a real studio and built the loft, walls, sinks, lighting, and our screenprinting table, all of which would be required for our printing processes.

"The Landland studio doubles as a fully functional screenprinting shop, focusing on record sleeves, posters, and art prints. We create our visuals and bring our ideas to life through screenprinting, with the aid of computers, scanners, photocopiers, drawings, etc.

"We screenprint all our posters ourselves, which is a really inexpensive way to end up with a stack of printed work. To set up your own screenprinting studio, all you really need is a lamp, a bathtub (or sinks), a table to print on, and a screen. For the Built To Spill poster we used transparent inks to create additional colors when different layers overlap. Each color is printed separately, so more colors equals higher costs. In this situation, we printed four colors (brown, light blue, green, and a very transparent gray), but with all of the overlapping combinations, it looks like a whole lot more."

LANDLAND
USA

COLORED PAPER

Fleming Design kept costs to an absolute minimum in creating this program by using colored paper that the printer had left over from a previous job. It was printed in one spot color, but twice, to increase the intensity of the black., As the original found paper was matte, the second hit of ink created a satin effect without incurring the costs of varnishing.

FLEMING DESIGN
CANADA

In nearly all cases of promotional printed literature, the work will be printed onto white paper; it might be gloss, silk, or matte, but it will be white. When was the last time you chose anything other than white as the bulk print stock? Is white paper stock always the best choice?

White paper with spot colors has been the industry standard for decades. If you want your next marketing piece to really stand out, consider using color printing on colored paper.

When you design for printing on colored paper, remember that conventional litho printing inks are transparent, not solid. This isn't apparent when you print on white paper, but you'll notice that images

or text printed on a cream-colored paper seem warmer; this is because the yellow tint of the paper shows through.

The darker the paper, the greater the effect on the color in your images. Prior to printing onto colored paper, ask your printer to advise you about dot gain. This is the term used to describe ink seeping into the paper fibers and spreading. This is most prevalent with colored papers, which are often uncoated and very soft in nature.

It's quite rare to see work printed on colored paper. Give it a go. It may just end up being the best thing you have printed in a long time.

TIP

Paper manufacturers are always very keen to promote their colored paper ranges. Go online to find who supplies paper to your country and call them. Most manufacturers have a dedicated sample-request team who will be delighted to send you samples of different colored papers in a range of sizes. These will be delivered direct to your door, usually within two to three days. Remember, it is a sample line—don't ask for or expect to get 500 sheets!

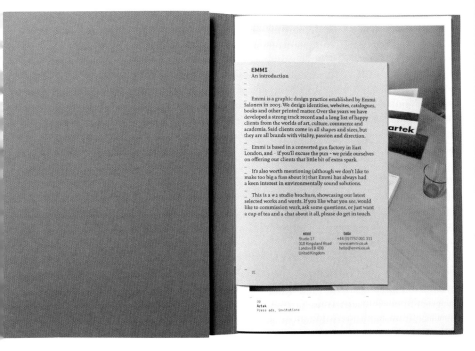

‹ The die-cuts on the cover of EMMI's self-
∨ promotional brochure allow extra sheets to be slotted into place. The colored stock brings vibrancy to the cover, without using printed inks. This reduces the need for extra plates during the printing process and therefore reduces costs. The brochure is divided into three sections: one-color pages in the front talk about the studio, the middle section features work in full color, on slightly larger sheets, and a one-color back section concentrates on case studies and client testimonials.

STUDIO EMMI
UK

> The challenge for design studio Young was to create a set of fliers at minimal cost, but with each one individual. The print is one-color on colored paper. Changing the paper color each time saves on printing costs, and has become a trademark for the events.

Don't be put off printing on colored papers by uncertainty. Most paper companies keep a range of samples of printing on their own colored stocks and will be eager to show you this. Get a paper rep to visit you—they will be delighted to do so. Your rep might leave you their book showing various effects (duotones, for instance) on particular colored stocks. You might even be able to get them to negotiate a discount for a specific paper stock for your in-house desktop printer.

An alternative to using the color of the underlying stock to influence the printed color is to use underprinting. Show-through can be alleviated by underprinting a base opaque white; this will neutralize the colored stock only where you then overprint.

For example, if you underprint an opaque white on a portion, or even all, of a colored sheet and then, once this has dried, print your duotone or full-color set over the white, the image will appear to jump off the page. The underprinting of white will give it an extra vibrancy, giving the image an enhanced depth.

YOUNG
UK

EDHV
THE NETHERLANDS

> Clever use of a single spot color on colored paper gives these fliers by Edhv striking depth and standout, but requires only a small print budget.

CASE STUDY:
HEY STUDIO

The aim of this branding project for Intermón Oxfam was to renew the image of Oxfam in Spain and create an emotional link between the association and its younger target market

To create the most visual impact, Barcelona-based Hey took letters and converted them into illustrations. Titles are reduced to a single word to communicate quickly and more directly.

The striking effect was created with a single special spot black printed directly onto various-colored papers. This helped keep the costs down, without losing any of the impact required.

CASE STUDY:
DONUTS

Brussels-based Donuts went to extreme lengths to create a fabulous collection of pages printed on colored stock for their art book about David de Tscharner.

The book was constructed entirely by hand in Donuts' studio using their own copiers and digital printers. Sheets of paper of various colors were run through the copiers, turned over, and fed back through to print on the reverse and create printed signatures. The sheets were then cropped down by hand to remove the outer edges and trim marks, allowing the printed pages to bleed. The sheets were then folded by hand and bound using canvas tape, section by section. This allows for additional sections to be added at any time in the future and to make any changes as and when required. Most importantly, it worked out to be a very cost-effective way of creating colorful brochures.

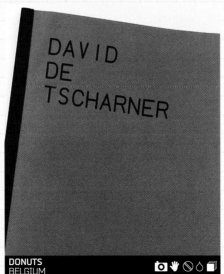

eps51 wanted to create a self-promotional poster/brochure at as low a cost as possible. They printed a single spot color onto colored paper and cross-folded the sheets to create the desired effect.

EPS51
GERMANY

The idea behind this project by DC Works was to Xerox directly onto colored paper. It is basic, cheap, eye-catching, and simple to produce—it has maximum impact with minimum costs.

DC WORKS
THE NETHERLANDS

ALTERNATIVES TO ART

The Nightingale and Rose By Oliver Rudland

Double Bill

B&W STUDIO
UK

Stripping a project right back to its core message, you may find it unnecessary to sweat over finding the perfect image. If it is simply an arbitrary graphic, then it's not really serving any purpose. Look at the text you have. Is it suitable to break up into large and small paragraphs and to play with the typography?

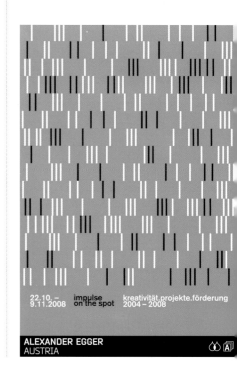

ALEXANDER EGGER
AUSTRIA

∧ For this poster, the typography has become the graphic. With clever use of letterspacing, leading, and choice of font, this proves that a good piece of design does not always need a visual graphic.

➤ In this poster the designer has removed every visual element and replaced it with simple black and white vertical dashes to create an intriguing and strong design.

Creating beauty from words alone is the sign of a really skilled designer. Look into the history of design and you'll find fantastic examples of typographic art. Bauhaus, El Lissitzky, Moholy-Nagy, de Stijl, Tschichold, and the Swiss typography movement all helped encourage typographic experimentation and promote the idea of using type alone to create powerful graphics. All through the twentieth century and into the twenty-first, fashions and styles can be dated by their typographic trends and styles; every era has its own look and its own heroes of typography.

The secret to great typography is to find your own influences and inspirations; look at how words flow, look at their angles, sizes, and styles, and how they work when they are brought together.

Look at bringing in blocks of solid color, knock the text out of some of these blocks, overlay text, and start to build up and layer your image. Designers need to learn how to manipulate color as well as typography and learn how the two can interact for maximum effect. Remember that different colors can have different effects; reds, for example, are usually regarded as warm, active, exciting (and dangerous!); blues and greens as cool and soothing.

> Studio Astrid Stavro created this series of affordable, but highly collectible artists' monographs as postcards, booklets, and posters all sold at the museum shop of the Ediciones de La Central. Imagery was replaced by classical typesetting and color, which allows the letters themselves to become the artwork.

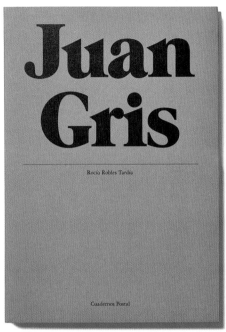

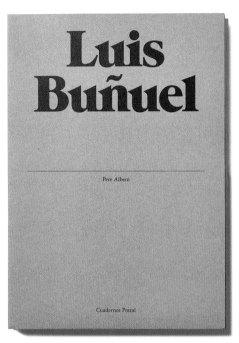

STUDIO ASTRID STAVRO
SPAIN

CASE STUDY:
LEWIS MOBERLY

The challenge with this design for upmarket supermarket chain Waitrose was to provide a powerful creative concept, uniting a visually eclectic range of 58 products, sold in a variety of pack structures and sizes, and to do so cost-effectively.

The labels feature a strong typographic style, which helped unify the diverse range of packaging. The subtle use of color enhances the appearance of the products, suggesting clean, fresh taste. The phrase on each label ("A dash of this," "A drizzle of that") reflects the gusto and informality of confident cooks.

Where possible, transparent packaging was chosen to show the product. This provides additional color, shape, and texture. The combination of typography and transparent packs meant that no money was spent on illustrating or photographing the products.

The design concept has now been extended to home-baking ingredients, fresh herbs, and ethnic ingredients.

LEWIS MOBERLY
UK

STUDIO INTERNATIONAL
CROATIA

‹ *Oprosti* (Forgive) was made for the Pope's arrival in Croatia. Printed in two spot colors, these very simple posters proved a massive hit in Croatia and were voted Croatia's poster of the year. Billboard rental and print production were supplied free of charge as the nation got behind this positive message of hope.

TIP

Different countries and cultures place different meanings on color. In Western countries black is the color of death and mourning; in China it is white. In India blue is associated with Krishna and is therefore a very positive color, while red is the color of purity and is used for weddings. In many other countries the "wedding color" is white. Purples and very dark blues have royal connotations in the West, while the equivalent in many Asian countries is yellow.

‹ Promotional material for La Chapelle du Geneteil.
⌄ The straightforward graphic-meets-typography approach, with printing in solid spot black, removed the need for photography and illustration—the type *is* the illustration. Ongoing for several years, this approach has delighted the exhibition's visitors, and its cost-saving techniques have delighted the client.

DONUTS
BELGIUM

CASE STUDY:
SOLAR INITIATIVE

EUROPE HAS A NEW DESIGN EVENT: FREEDESIGNDOM

IN SEPTEMBER AND OCTOBER 2008, UNDER THE NAME FOUR WEEKS OF FREEDESIGNDOM, THE DUTCH CITIES OF AMSTERDAM AND UTRECHT WILL HOST A WIDE VARIETY OF INTERNATIONAL DESIGN AND FASHION EVENTS FOR A BROAD AUDIENCE.

THE PROGRAMME INCLUDES VIA MILANO NEW DUTCH DESIGN (A SHOWCASE OF NEW WORK), STREETLAB (AN EXCITING FESTIVAL OF STREET FASHION AND DESIGN); MULTIPLICITY & VISUAL IDENTITIES (A CONFERENCE ON DESIGN RESEARCH IN MULTICULTURAL SOCIETIES), THE WOONBEURS AMSTERDAM HOME SHOW, THE POPULAR INSIDE DESIGN AMSTERDAM EXHIBITION, AND A SYMPOSIUM ON SOCIAL DESIGN FROM LEADING-EDGE DESIGN ORGANISATION UTRECHT MANIFEST.

DURING FOUR WEEKS OF FREEDESIGNDOM, AMSTERDAM WILL ALSO HOST, FOR THE FIRST TIME, EXPERIMENTADESIGN. STARTING IN 2008, THIS INNOVATIVE, MULTIDISCIPLINARY EVENT, FOUNDED IN LISBON, WILL TAKE PLACE ALTERNATELY IN LISBON AND AMSTERDAM. THE EXPERIMENTADESIGN AMSTERDAM BIENNALE CONSISTS OF EXHIBITIONS, CONFERENCES, 'OPEN TALKS', AND SIDE EVENTS TAKING PLACE AT UNUSUAL LOCATIONS THROUGHOUT THE CITY.

WITH ITS WIDE-RANGING PROGRAMME, FREEDESIGNDOM IS A MAJOR NEW EVENT ON THE INTERNATIONAL CREATIVE CALENDAR, HELD ANNUALLY IN AMSTERDAM AND UTRECHT.

premsela
.org/   Ministerie van Economische Zaken

FOUR WEEKS OF FREEDESIGNDOM
PRINSES IRENESTRAAT 19 / 1077 WT AMSTERDAM / THE NETHERLANDS
P.O. BOX 75905 / 1070 AX AMSTERDAM / THE NETHERLANDS
INFO@FREEDESIGNDOM.COM / FREEDESIGNDOM.COM

SOLAR INITIATIVE
THE NETHERLANDS

Freedesigndom is a month-long design festival, held in Amsterdam and Utrecht, in which existing exhibitions and new design-related events are brought together in a single exhibition.

Netherlands-based Solar Initiative created the overall identity for the festival and worked this into the main graphic elements. This allowed for a design that didn't favor one discipline over another. The black dots could be used as stickers to contain a series of typographic messages, but they always had to appear in groups, never on their own. The result was a form of branding unique to the exhibition and easily recognized. At the same time it was very cost-effective and easy to implement.

> A typographic option is probably one of the cheapest design solutions possible. There is nothing better than a design that screams at you. Paul Snowden's designs for record/CD sleeves for Universal Music, Funk Mundial, and Boys Noize Records certainly achieve this.

PAUL SNOWDEN
BERLIN

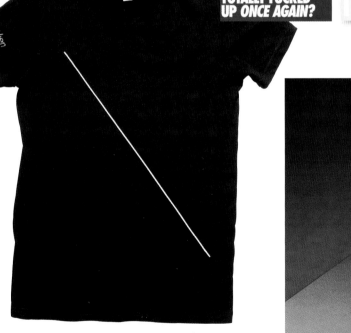

❯ Traffic Design Consultants created this alcohol screening pack for the UK's National Health Service and brought the job in under budget by scrapping images and, instead, taking the two main corporate colors and house fonts to create a series of strong typographic images.

TRAFFIC DESIGN CONSULTANTS
UK

CHRISTOF NARDIN
AUSTRIA

^ Even a basic line can create an interesting graphic, as proven by this simple, yet elegant T-Shirt design.

ARCHIVE YOUR WORK

There is a strong belief among designers that a good idea deserves to, and will eventually, see the light of day.

It might not be exactly what the client initially had in mind, but that's not to say it won't be perfect for a job in the future... even for a different client. It's not about carrying around a bag of ideas hoping for a client to buy into them, it's simply that if you have invested time (blood, sweat, and tears) in an idea that you know has longevity and originality, it's worth hanging on to on the off-chance.

The key thing is never to throw away good work. You should keep all your ideas to hand and look back on them now and then to see where and when they can be used. You can still be just as ruthless with what you actually present to a client. This is very important if you find yourself doing a lot of pitching against other agencies where the tender requires a visual input as well as costings. A lot of time and money can be saved by reusing templates and presentation styles, especially if there is also a request for a written presentation outlining your experience, resources, and what value you are able to bring to the client.

The obvious benefit of a comprehensive and clear filing system is that it will save you valuable time (and therefore money) in the future if you find yourself trying to reproduce something similar when the appropriate circumstance presents itself. There is no point reinventing the wheel each time. Cut down on your search time by giving your file and folder names adequately descriptive titles. Many design companies now run a central server system on which all company work is stored at the one location, with no jobs actually existing on individuals' computers. Without damaging the original work, this is a great "hunting ground" to recycle and rework older ideas that never got to final production.

TIP

Not all designers can afford to stack their studio shelves with the latest design books. However, thanks to the freedom granted by the Internet, you can build up a digital library of visuals by your favorite creatives using the scrapbooking method. Simply drag, drop, and store. Many websites selling books (Amazon, Play, etc.), will actually show you various pages inside a book. This can provide a means of quickly referencing anything from an unusual format to a typographic treatment.

TIP

Create a folder on your computer into which you can drag and drop anything that sparks your imagination when doing the rounds of your favorite blogs or design websites. Your computer's screensaver preferences may then allow you to turn this folder into a slideshow of your favorite images, which will start to roll whenever your computer is idle for a designated period of time. This is good for inspiration, looks fantastic when you are not at your desk, and adds visual variety to your studio.

‹ Use a sensible filing system to catalog
^ past projects, with a designated space
for development work.

CHAPTER 3:
SOURCING

LUNDGREN+LINDQVIST
SWEDEN

THE LAW

FLÁVIO HOBO
PORTUGAL

▲ Poster for a puppet show performed by
Duo Anfíbios from Brazil. The aim of this project
was to promote the new show called "Sonhos
de um Pinguim de Geladeira" (Dreams of a Fridge
Penguin). To produce the booklet and poster
within budget, Flávio Hobo used downloaded
free fonts (Andes and Anagram), and worked
with 90gsm low-cost paper. The booklet was
produced in four languages: English, French,
Portuguese, and Spanish.

**Be very, very careful when downloading
anything, text or imagery, especially
from the Internet. You are entering
a legal minefield.**

Very few of us will ever be sued. Even
if action is sanctioned, removing the
work can often resolve the situation. The
problem arises when large multinationals
run global campaigns and make massive
profits using text or imagery not fully
copyright-cleared. If you are in any doubt,
do not download and use material! If you
can, check with a lawyer before using
anything that isn't fully copyright-cleared;
if you can't, don't use it.

COPYRIGHT

Copyright protects the right of the legal
party in the contract (author, photographer,
artist, or publisher) to control the use of
the work being reproduced. There are
international agreements governing this.
However, in the Internet age, intellectual
property rights are an increasingly complex
area, and local legislative systems are
often at odds with the global, file-sharing
impetus of the Internet.

Remember, even if you do have copyright
approval, it may only be for that one job.
If you commission a reprint six months
later, remember, you may not have
clearance for a second run.

CREATIVE COMMONS

Creative Commons is a relatively new
approach to copyright. Conceived in
2001, it provides a platform for people
who are happy for their work to be used
for nonprofit or educational projects free
of charge, as long as the work is credited
to them. It basically offers "Some Rights
Reserved" as an alternative to the usual
"All Rights Reserved" terms of traditional
copyright. There are several alternative
licenses that permit different levels of
usage. To find out more, take a look
at the creative Commons website
www.creativecommons.org.

➤ This artwork was created for I Was a Dog,
an exhibition at the Wrocław Gallery of
Contemporary Art in Poland. The inspiration
was vintage photography from the NASA
collection and the story of the two Soviet space
dogs, Laika and Strelka. Copyright-free images
were downloaded and the font Mod, designed
by Bulgarian Svetoslav Simov, was downloaded
free from Fontfabric.

TIP:

Always read the terms and conditions of copyright restrictions before downloading and using shots or vector artwork from free or pay-to-use sites. Clearance is usually granted automatically, but some artwork comes with restrictions. Is there a restriction on the print run, the time period for which the shot can be used, or the geographical area in which it can be reproduced or distributed, and does the original creator insist that their work is credited to them in a specific way? Never presume that because you have paid a small amount to download something or sourced it from a free site, it is actually safe to use it. Check each site and each image's terms of use individually.

TIP: A TRUE STORY

A reputable and well-established firm paid for an inexpensive website to be created online, outside their home country. They didn't speak to anyone direct, nor did they have any involvement in its construction. They simply sent all text for the site by e-mail. The final website was very poor, but at least it was live and online. One year after the site was completed, the firm whose site it was received notification of pending legal action over a photograph that had been used without permission. The shot in question had been taken from a photographer's website without clearance to do so. The firm had assumed the site was created using copyright-free images. They were now being sued for £2,000—the site had only cost them £300. Attempts to contact the website's builders led to a dead end—they had vanished. In the end the firm settled out of court on a payment of £500 and the removal of the shot from the site. It was an expensive lesson not just in cost, but also in time.

CITYABYSS
POLAND

FREE & BUDGET FONTS

Choosing the right font can be crucial in the making or breaking of great design. With an almost endless list of perfectly cut serifs, sans serifs, funky comic-book fonts, and quirky dingbats, there is sure to be a perfectly suited font for any given brief, no matter how obscure. So, where can one obtain such fonts, or more importantly, where can one affordably obtain such fonts?

There are masses of fantastic free font sites on the web, but a note of warning before you download—not all of the fonts available are free for professional use, and often they are very poorly cut, which can have horrendous consequences. However, with a sharp eye, you should be able to separate the imposters from the real deal. Look out for poor automatic letterspacing, lazily drawn ascenders and descenders, or simply uneven edges and poorly rounded curves. With careful selection it should be relatively easy to find almost any style, shape, and weight of typeface you desire.

Free fonts can provide fantastic alternatives for certain jobs, particularly logo designs. Logos rely on being a stand-alone marque or identity with unique features and color schemes—using a standard system font or an everyday font for a logo will make it feel bland and easy to copy. Dingbats can also provide the basis for logos as they're essentially free vectors that can be manipulated endlessly to create the new pictorial element for your logo.

Most design studios will purchase fonts or font libraries direct from the manufacturers. Although the cost of this can run into thousands, it does give the designer access to all the classic fonts (legally!) and allows design studios to get on with their daily work without the disruption of having to source a certain typeface should a client's corporate guidelines require it. Font manufacturers include Linotype, The Font Bureau, Monotype, ITC (International Typeface Corporation), Adobe, T.26, etc.

Experiment with fonts: buy some, download some free, and use them together for the best results.

Some free fonts have usage restrictions that allow for personal use only, excluding use for profit-making commercial use. This should be explained in any terms and conditions accompanying the font, which we strongly advise you to read before downloading anything. Be careful. Using fonts illegally is a form of theft. If you are creating material for others and you are profiting from this, you will need commercial licensing.

A lot of free fonts don't include the special and extended characters that come with the commercial version. You may get the regular and light cuts, but what if you need a bold or italic? You may find you have to buy these, and that's when the initial offer of a free font has done its job and roped you in.

SVETOSLAV SIMOV
BULGARIA

^ Mod is an original, experimental font that
< is applicable for any type of graphic design—web, print, motion graphics, etc. Designed by Svetoslav Simov; downloaded from Fontfabric free of charge.

TIP

Most computers come with a decent number of free fonts installed, allowing you to start working straight away. If you are on a limited budget, build up your font library gradually. Quite often, design studios charge a little bit extra on every large job and use this money to buy a new typeface, initially for use on that job, but later to become a studio font for all to use. There are certain fonts you simply won't be able to live without, Helvetica, Arial, Times, and Swiss among them.

Free fonts may not be as well produced as commercial fonts. This could lead to production problems; remember, what you see on-screen isn't necessarily what prints out. Always check that the font has dashes, commas, and question marks included. You will be amazed how many free fonts don't have ligatures, punctuation marks, or even numbers.

Another thing to check is what format these fonts are in, and whether they will open on your computer or be read by your font-management system. Fonts can come in TrueType, PostScript, OpenType, etc. Today, most fonts are universal, but older fonts created for the Apple Macintosh won't work on a Microsoft PC. Always check whether the font you are proposing can be used on both Mac and PC.

Never download a font from an unknown source or "homemade" site. On top of the possibility of downloading a virus, some commercial fonts are made available with no indication that they are not actually free fonts. This will place you in breach of copyright, and you probably won't be able to find where the font came from in order to source it legally. Download only from sites that are genuine.

The following list is simply a starting point for sourcing fonts—there are plenty more sites out there.

www.dafont.com
An archive of freely downloadable fonts. Categorized by theme, the fonts can also be sorted by name, date, and popularity. A highly praised site

www.fontfreak.com/pre.htm
One of the largest and most frequently visited freeware font sites on the net. A "must visit" site

www.1001freefonts.com
A strong collection of freeware fonts and dingbats, all listed with the creator's permission, so they come copyright-cleared

www.fontsearchengine.com
This useful site offers over 10,000 free fonts and features a search engine, so you can quickly find what you need. Font Search Engine also includes a database of free font archives, font utilities, and a roundup of free font designers

www.fontface.com
A highly rated site for those in search of the latest free fonts on the web

www.highfonts.com
Offers over 3,000 fonts, all organized alphabetically and with preview ability

www.typenow.net
Over 5,000 free fonts and dingbats for both Windows and Mac

www.urbanfonts.com
Over 8,000 free fonts and dingbats for PC and Mac, sorted alphabetically

www.007fonts.com
Fonts in TrueType (.ttf) format, sorted alphabetically. It's possible to preview each font and download in ZIP format

www.1-800-fonts.com
As with 007, fonts are in TrueType (.ttf) format, sorted alphabetically

www.abstractfonts.com
A massive site containing over 12,000 free fonts listed by category, designer, popularity, etc.

www.acidfonts.com
4,000 freeware fonts and dingbats for Windows and Mac

www.bvfonts.com
A broad selection of TrueType fonts listed by category

www.searchfreefonts.com
Over 13,000 free fonts for download. Includes a search engine for finding what you need

www.fontsy.com
4,000 freeware fonts and dingbats

www.fontsforflash.com
As the domain name suggests, this site offers a smaller selection of fonts suitable for use in Macromedia Flash

www.webfxmall.com/fonts
A good collection featuring many fonts not available on other sites

www.jabroo.com
This site features 16,000 free fonts, and an online custom graphics generator

BENDER, BLACK
ABCDEFGHIJKLMNOPQRSTUVWXYZ
abcdefghijklmnopqrstuvwxyz
1234567890!@#$%^&*()

Designed by Ivan Gladkikh, Oleg Zhuravlev

MUSEO, 300
ABCDEFGHIJKLMNOPQRSTUVWXYZ
abcdefghijklmnopqrstuvwxyz
1234567890!@#$%^&*()

Designed by Jos Buivenga

CREATING FONTS

Every now and again the huge list of pre-installed fonts on your system just won't provide what you want for a job. If you would like to create your own font, but are worried that this is simply too difficult, there are a handful of fantastic free font-designer web applications, including FontStruct and Fontifier.

▼ Drahtzieher Design & Kommunikation created their own typeface, Strangelove, and used it throughout magazine *Tanz & Archive*.

FontStruct
fontstruct.fontshop.com

FontStruct is a free font-building tool created by world-leading retailer of digital type, FontShop. FontStruct lets you create fonts quickly and easily from geometrical shapes arranged in a grid pattern, like tiles or bricks. You can fill out one key letter or a whole font, distribute your creation freely or with rights reserved, and offer it up as an easy-to-install TrueType font. Using FontStruct's tools requires a free sign-up, or you could just browse FontStruct's library of original fonts for download. FontStruct is free to use online.

Fontifier
www.fontifier.com

Fontifier is an inexpensive application that will turn your handwriting into a reusable typeface. Start by printing out the Fontifier template, then create your font by writing it down on the template and scanning it. Upload and preview the template. If you're satisfied, pay a small fee and download your font. This can be used just like a regular font and is fully compatible with all applications.

Fontographer
www.fontlab.com/font-editor/fontographer

Macromedia Fontographer is the easiest application with which to create royalty-free fonts for print, multimedia, and the Internet. With it you can easily expand existing fonts to create lighter or heavier versions of your fonts or include fractions, symbols, foreign characters, and logos in Type 1, Type 3, and TrueType fonts. You can also create an entire typeface from scratch. Fonts created with Fontographer can be used in any program with a font menu, on Windows and Macintosh platforms.

You can scan in a signature, autotrace it, and create a font from it, or blend any two fonts to create a completely new font. The software isn't free, but it is relatively simple to use.

DRAHTZIEHER DESIGN & KOMMUNIKATION
AUSTRIA

Text: Wolfgang Beinhard
Illustration: Christian Pearstein

46

In seiner Jugend hatte es sich Georg angewöhnt, die Fleischbrocken ohne langes Kauen hinunterzuschlucken. Es saßen damals mit dem Vater und den drei Brüdern vier Nahrungskonkurrenten am Familientisch; schlechte Voraussetzungen, um jeden Bissen hinreichend zu kauen und einzuspeicheln.

Fast jeden Tag gab es in Georgs Familie Fleisch. Ein Mittagessen ohne Fleisch wurde nicht als ein solches angesehen. Nur freitags gab es meistens eine Süßspeise oder irgendwelche Teiggerichte. Immerhin servierte die Mutter dann stets eine Fleischsuppe als Vorspeise.

Den Fleischnachschub besorgte man sich aus unterschiedlichen Quellen. Da gab es vor allem die zwei Metzgereien, in denen der Vater Handel trieb, und bei welchen man regelmäßig Fleisch- und Wurstwaren einkaufte.

Einen Teil des Fleischverzorns der wöchentlichen Familie eroberte man durch eine kleine Eigenproduktion.

Georgs Eltern hielten immer eine große Anzahl Kleinvieh, Hasen, Truthähne, und vor allem Hühner; in allen Größen und Farben. Hinter dem Haus befand sich die Stadt und die einzige Freilandhühnerhaltung die ganzen Fleisch. Insbesondere die Hühner...

Herr Fleisch und die Hühner der Mutter

47

CHRISTOF NARDIN
AUSTRIA

La ndjager

Fleisch

Landjäger No.3

> Christof Nardin has created several of his own typefaces and used them throughout his design work in an almost fine-art manner.

TRANSFER STUDIO
UK

> This self-initiated piece was created after a hard-disk breakdown meant that months of work was lost forever. Inspired by what was left, Transfer Studio developed an entire typeface; a process that worked as a course of constructive healing. The screenprinted T-shirt was limited to a special edition of 50. The packaging was screenprinted directly onto an off-the-shelf postal box, in one color.

HAND-DRAWN TYPE

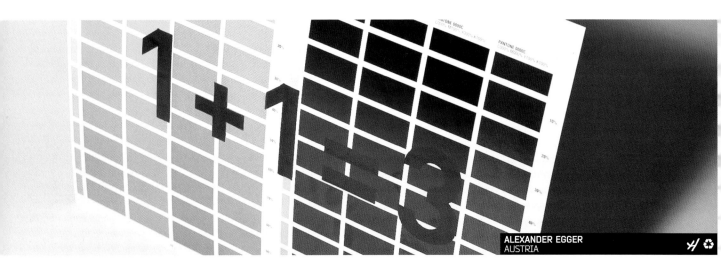

ALEXANDER EGGER
AUSTRIA

Hand-drawn lettering has become increasingly popular with young designers who enjoy the freedom of drawing a typeface to give a project a specific feel.

It is rare to see a large corporate client go for hand-drawn text as part of their corporate look, but it can be used to soften a document and make it more accessible, especially if it is aimed at a younger, trendier audience.

While using hand-drawn fonts will not necessarily save you money on the type front, it will help you create a specific mood or feel, and it can save you money on the image front—the hand-drawn fonts often become focal points in themselves and can take the place of images or illustrations. A design based around a hand-drawn font can create a statement, sit outside the "norm," and simply give a job a unique look and feel.

You are more likely to use a hand-drawn font as a graphic than an actual font. Once it has been set up as a font that you can type on your keyboard, it will become more regimented and lose its appeal. It is better to hand-draw each sentence, paragraph, or heading, scan it in, color it up, and drop it into your document as a TIFF file. That way you can move it about for positioning purposes without losing creative freedom.

Research this online, look at other people's hand-drawn fonts, and at how they have used these in their designs, then have a go yourself. It's a lot of fun and can yield some fantastic results.

^ This limited-edition set of 250 exhibition invitations was handmade with stencil and marker fonts printed over the top of color test-pattern sheets already printed for a previous job.

LETTERFORMS
COMPOSED
OF LOCAL
CHARACTER
AND
ARCHITECTURAL
DETAIL.

^
> Self-promotional mailer for London-based
Blacklabs. Printed one spot color onto Arjo
Wiggins Hi Speed Opaque 80gsm to allow for
cross-folding. Blacklabs took elements from
local architecture, photographing these, then
sketching them by hand back at the studio,
"weaving" them into typographic forms.

BLACKLABS
UK

CASE STUDY:
TRANSFORMER

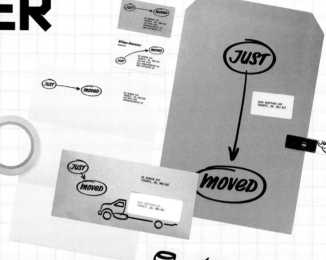

Just Moved is a Canadian low-cost, full-service, local and national residential moving company. The main goal for Moscow's Transformer Studio was to create an identity that reflects ease of movement and affordability of services.

This identity is deliberately cheap to reproduce in printed format, but it is not low in quality. The logo itself reflects simplicity and affordability.

Most production involved printing in one spot color and with no graphics other than those hand-drawn or created in-house. The graphics could not be simpler and in keeping it this way the product and its brand values are easier for the public to grasp and therefore buy into.

TRANSFORMER STUDIO
RUSSIA

TRAFFIC DESIGN CONSULTANTS
UK

‹ *Young Voices* is a quarterly community youth magazine. Created for a local nonprofit organization, there is no budget to commission anything directly. For the cover of this edition, designer Gordon Beveridge hand-drew all the titles of the featured articles. These were then scanned into Photoshop, and dropped onto a photograph of an old wooden school desk.

ARNAUD
FRANCE

‹ Arnaud Design created this wonderful CD packaging from hand-drawn illustrations and fonts colored up to create a strong and memorable piece of packaging.

ALEXANDER EGGER
AUSTRIA

▲ The logo for Red-hot, a small communications and marketing agency based in Vienna, had to suggest innovation, creativity, and competence. It consists of two elements: the printed "r" and an underscore that leaves a blank area, which has to be written in to complete the logo.

❯ For this invitation to the book presentation of 360° Design Austria, the names of all the institutions represented were handwritten on the basic layout of the promotional posters.

Hand-drawn fonts can add impact and allow for total creative freedom. This has been well thought through on these teen-based sexual health posters by Socio Design.

CREATING VECTOR ILLUSTRATIONS

A vector image is a graphic that has been created in a drawing program (such as Adobe Illustrator, Macromedia FreeHand, or CorelDRAW). It uses paths to create polygons or lines and stores information mathematically. Vector art is resolution-independent, which means that, no matter whether you enlarge or shrink the image, the output quality will remain the same.

SCALE TO FIT
THE NETHERLANDS

❮ Night of Comedy is a group of talented comedians playing to theaters across the Netherlands. This identity shows its diversity, enthusiasm, and, of course, fun. The vector artwork created could then be used by each comedian to show what his act is all about.

SICKSYSTEMS
RUSSIA

❮ For the new Moscow Nike store SickSystems created a series of vector images, posters, fliers, and sculptures, which ended up appearing in street culture–related blogs and sites worldwide.

Creating your own vector-based artwork is an excellent way to guarantee the originality of your work. It gives you control over how it looks, from the line style you select to the colors you use. It also gives you the freedom to chop and change it when you want to. It may even be possible (client allowing) to then sell your vector illustration to others through sites such as iStockphoto.

You can buy in vector artwork, or you can create your own. It's not that difficult, but you need to decide how best to spend your time. Will the client thank you for an original piece of artwork in their design and feel that the time spent is justified, or will they happily go for an image purchased from the web?

You could spend a full day creating your vector illustration compared with an hour searching online for similar, but not exclusive, imagery. There are advantages and disadvantages in both options. Is it worth the risk of creating a concept based around an image that is available to everyone? A third alternative is to mix and match, creating your own artwork to use alongside elements of stock artwork.

Creating a bank of vector imagery could give you all the illustrations you need to roll out a client's campaign over a long time period, releasing a new vector image every week or month, etc., or to populate the pages of a multisection report for which multiple graphics are required.

❮ For this nonprofit initiative, costs needed to be kept to a minimum. All design and development time was given free, and the designers created vector illustrations that could be used on all elements, from posters to websites.

THE HOUSE LONDON
UK

CASE STUDY:
TRAFFIC

In a cost-cutting exercise and to provide the client with marketing material for several years, Glasgow-based Traffic Design Consultants first created a large number of vector male and female illustrations before a single brochure had been designed.

H4U (Health for you), a Glasgow-based youth support and health organisation part-funded by the National Health Service, wanted a range of literature that 10–19 year-olds would respond to and not be embarrassed to be seen reading. With a limited budget the client would require numerous different leaflets, zip banners, promotional giveaways, web sites, etc.

After several meetings and steering groups with local teenage youth clubs, the favoured route was upbeat colors with vector illustrations. It was decided that Traffic would produce a large bank of stand-alone male and female illustrations that could then be called upon over several years to create various pieces of literature. Senior Designer Gordon Beveridge chose to create all illustrations himself (for continuity) using Adobe Illustrator. Only when all these illustrations had been approved by the teenage steering group (representing a cross section of the young community) did any design work actually start for the proposed printed literature. Figures show that this has been a hugely successful campaign with most local teenagers being aware of H4U's existence.

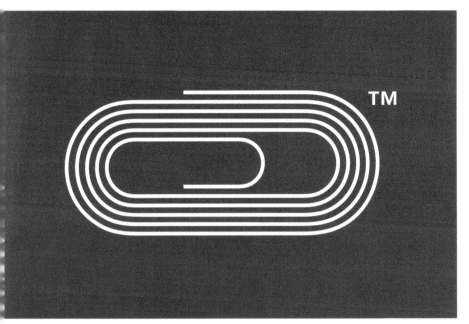

> ⌄ The Richard House Children's Hospice charity helps make life easier for terminally ill children and their families. Their Office Games aims to bring office and sport together to create a unique contest. Events include: Floppy Discus, Office Chair Relay, Recycling Rowing, and Post-it Note Fencing. The designers chose a vector route to answer the brief. The humble paperclip became the heart of the identity, creating the main running-track logo and a set of icons depicting each sporting event. Bold use of the core red gave a cost-effective way of achieving maximum impact. One-color posters, T-shirts, and pop-up stands kept the costs down.

THE PARTNERS
UK

BUYING VECTOR ILLUSTRATIONS

Purchasing vector artwork can save you many hours of design time and there is absolutely no reason why you can't then edit what you've bought to add new dimensions and elements.

In some ways this has evolved from clip art to something far more dynamic. Free or inexpensive vector artwork is readily available. Some sites are free and some require a small payment per download, while others even ask for a donation at the discretion of the designer. It is vital that you check all terms, conditions, and legal restrictions on any files you download from the web, either free or for a small fee.

Below is a small list of sites worth visiting, but there are many more!

www.123freevectors.com
www.coolvectors.com
www.createsk8.com
www.dezignus.com
www.flavafx.com
www.freevectors.net
www.istockphoto.com
www.keepdesigning.com
www.qvectors.com
www.vecteezy.com
www.vector4free.com
www.vectorart.org
www.vector-art.blogspot.com
www.vectorjungle.com
www.vectorportal.com
www.vectorvalley.com
www.vectorvault.com
www.vectorwallpapers.net
www.veeqi.com
www.vintagevectors.com

✔ This poster was produced using scanners, stock images, and free fonts. The final size was set so that two posters could fit on an Epson large-format printer.

ERIK BORRESON
USA

TRAFFIC DESIGN CONSULTANTS
UK

> Traffic Design Consultants needed access to high-quality vector images that could be downloaded fast and allow the designers to open the files, make structural and color-based changes, then manipulate these to work around the photography supplied by the client. Suitable images were found at www.istockphoto.com and downloaded for a small fee. The client was delighted with the finished brochure.

NOTE

It would be ill-advised to run a national campaign for a world-leading consumer product based around found or free downloaded imagery.

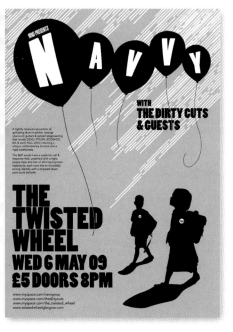

GORDON BEVERIDGE
UK

▲ This poster was created for live music venue The Twisted Wheel. Simple flat color was combined with hand-drawn fonts, and imagery sourced as free vector files.

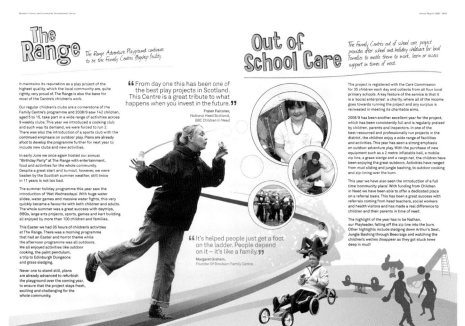

TRADITIONAL ILLUSTRATION

"Traditional illustration" can cover all forms of non-computer-generated drawing. An illustration is simply a visualization such as a drawing, painting, photograph, linocut, or any other artwork that stresses subject more than form.

The aim of an illustration is to inspire emotion in the viewer and, when used in conjunction with text, to expand on the linguistic aspects of the narrative. An illustration should add interest and form to a design.

Illustration within graphic design probably peaked in the 1970s and 1980s when nearly every design studio either had a large bank of freelance illustrators to call on or employed an in-house illustrator. By the 1990s, traditional illustrators found themselves challenged by those using computer software such as Adobe Illustrator and Photoshop. Designers found themselves, through the introduction of better software, increasingly capable of drawing and painting directly into a computer, speeding up the whole process and reducing the overall cost to the client. The dwindling budgets of the time encouraged this.

> The Ray™ campaign was produced to launch Allseating's newest chair design. The campaign Parcel developed focused on the story behind the design of the chair. This allowed Parcel to use the sketches produced by the industrial design team and minimize reliance on expensive photography. Parcel also saved on location and styling fees by holding the photo shoot in their own offices.

BASICS09
GERMANY

every detail tells a story.

PARCEL DESIGN
CANADA

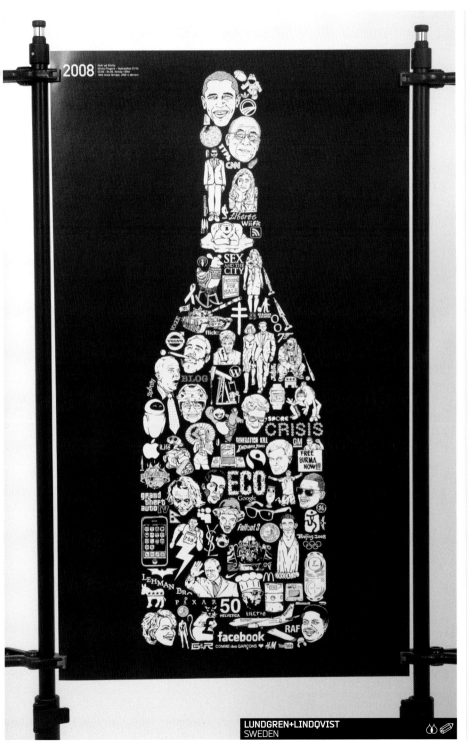

Today, many illustration students use this technology themselves, but with equal emphasis placed on more traditional techniques. As a result, traditional and digital techniques are often used together. Designers are merging the boundaries of fine and commercial art, using illustration with graphic design, typography, and photography. Specialist illustrators are now less common than they were, but can be highly sought after and often fully booked weeks in advance as designers scramble to get original illustrations they simply cannot get the right look for themselves. Qualified illustrators are using their digital and traditional skills in a way that is unique to them. There will always be a place for skilled illustrators in the design industry, but why not have a go yourself? After all, you are creative.

Starting can be as simple as buying a pencil and a sketchbook to see if you can still remember how to draw. Or buying a piece of scraperboard or lino from your local art store to try mimicking a woodcut or etching. Then, of course, you can scan it in and digitally enhance it.

‹ Lundgren+Lindqvist were approached to produce a poster for a big New Year's Eve party, but there was virtually no budget. They decided to summarize the year in pictures. Buying the licensed pictures was too expensive. The solution was to draw the 114 selected ideas by hand. Using only two colors lowered the printing costs.

LUNDGREN+LINDQVIST
SWEDEN

CASE STUDY:
344

Stefan G. Bucher is director of US design house 344, based in Los Angeles, and creator of the Monsters series.

Monsters was created on a shoestring budget in the designer/illustrator's own living room. Bucher used cheap ink on cheap paper, then shot the illustrations with a succession of cheap cameras. As the success of and hunger for Bucher's illustrations grew, he decided to create a commercial book, *100 Days of Monsters*. He also launched the massively popular Daily Monsters website, which has become a global phenomenon.

CITYABYSS
POLAND

❯ This work for OFFF, an international festival for post-digital creation, was inspired by the theme of the festival itself—this isn't flying, this is falling with style. The artwork is a mix of photography, typography, and hand-drawn illustrations by the designers.

DIGITAL ILLUSTRATION

Many digital artists produce their own work from the ground up, using public-domain imagery; clippings from old magazines, books, and family albums; and Polaroids, all blended with hand-drawn illustrations and typography. This collaging requires designers to be extremely resourceful and mindful of copyright restrictions, but it can be a cost-effective way of producing your own imagery. The list of avenues to explore for source material means that this remix approach can produce unique results.

Since the advent of affordable digital photography, taking your own photos has become an economical and quick means of getting an image in the style you want.

▾ *Decode Magazine* is an independent arts magazine from designer Gabriel Solomons. Many of the digital illustrations used in the magazine are donated free of charge by designers, illustrators, art students, and Solomons himself. This helps to keep the magazine free, but production values high.

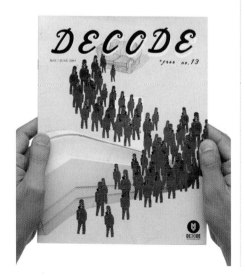

GABRIEL SOLOMONS
UK

deviantArt

deviantART is an online community that has showcased various forms of user-made artwork since its launch in 2000. Over 11 million members are responsible for the 100 million submissions, with around 100,000 new submissions daily. deviantART aims to provide a location for artists to exhibit and discuss their works. Artwork is organized according to a clear and concise category structure, including photography, digital art, traditional art, literature, Flash, and filmmaking. The site also offers extensive downloadable resources, including stock photography and tutorials.

The downloadable art is largely free, but terms and conditions regarding where and how the imagery can be reused vary across the content, dependent upon the artist. For some art a simple credit will suffice; other artists stipulate that their images should not be used for commercial projects. The stock imagery on offer is not all of a high standard, but there is enough that you stand a reasonable chance of finding what you are looking for.

The application resources offer countless brushes, actions, and patterns for Illustrator and Photoshop. A downside is that many of the layered Photoshop resources are poorly sized, which hints at a large number of hobbyists among the community's 11 million members. However, the multitude of tutorials, plug-ins, templates, patterns, actions, textures, and brushes makes deviantART, at the very least, a useful tool for producing digital illustrations.

Two posters by Lionel Scholtes of Graphic Diversion. All illustrations were digitally sourced from imagebanks. Scholtes then drew over the top using Adobe Illustrator, and added type.

DIY PHOTOGRAPHY

Personal work for Japanese designers Nam – The Graphic Collective. The concept for this project was to use props that were already in the studio, from the furniture to the coffee cup. The furniture was hung with gut wire and the model held by harness. The only computer retouching was to erase the gut and harness ropes.

NAM – THE GRAPHIC COLLECTIVE
JAPAN

Digital photography allows the user to view their photograph instantly, to download the file straight to computer or e-mail it direct to a colleague or friend, and to edit it. Digital technology has revolutionized photography, allowing amateur photographers far greater control over their files, removing costly processing fees, and bringing fast, powerful cameras into the price range of hobbyists.

Almost every design studio owns a digital SLR (DSLR) camera and a variety of lenses. Used well, a good DSLR can be worth its weight in gold. Save a fortune and do your own photography.

If you have a good eye for design, the chances are you have a good eye for balance and can take a reasonably good photograph. All you have to work out is what all the buttons on the camera do.

It's not really possible to advise on the best camera, as this will vary according to specific requirements, but like anything, buy the best you can afford. Get advice from chat forums and go to a large photographic stockist for a demonstration of the camera.

You won't create an in-house studio to rival a professional one, but you can save a lot of time and money by doing the simpler things yourself. Create your own lightbox, build up a corner of your room as a mini pack-shot studio with a white backdrop, invest in some good lamps for lighting, and don't forget a tripod—digital cameras are not forgiving of camera shake. Trial and error is a good way of getting the shots you need. Have a go. You may well surprise yourself.

Porter Novelli demonstrates beautifully the importance of creative freedom given by DIY photography. The setup and shooting of recyclable household packaging makes for a perfect cover and illustrations for the SCA Recycling brochure.

TIP

When buying a DSLR for design work, it is essential to invest in a good prime lens for everyday use. Typically, they give a slightly better image quality, and are lighter, cheaper, and smaller than a standard zoom lens of the same quality. Prime lenses also have a larger aperture than equivalent zoom lenses, so they are able to work better in conditions where the light is restricted. Another vital lens for the designer is a good macro lens for extreme close-up work. This is really important if you wish to take photographs of your own printed design work either for a digital portfolio or a website. A macro lens will allow you to zoom in so close to a piece of print that you can see the fibers of the paper or the embossing created on a foil block. Most macro lenses can focus to infinity, so they can also be used as a general-purpose lens.

PORTER NOVELLI
UK

CASE STUDY:
EXPOSURE BY DESIGN

The brief was to help create the start-up of a beauty salon on a shoestring budget. ebd (exposure by design) used in-house photography to reflect the owner's vision of a modern and edgy, but exceptional beauty-care service.

ebd created six core brand images and managed all production and photography themselves. The imagery had to be simple, free, and shot in a makeshift studio in ebd's own offices, all in a single day.

ebd also helped create the look and feel for both the in-store experience and the website.

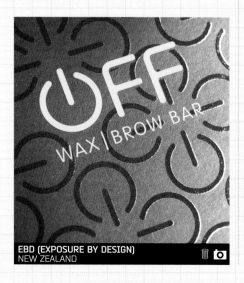

EBD (EXPOSURE BY DESIGN)
NEW ZEALAND

TIP
Fully loaded with features, DSLRs appeal to enthusiasts who are serious about their photography. With a good-quality lens being essential for good-quality photos, you need to make sure you leave enough in your budget to buy lenses as well as the camera body itself.

❮ Rinse is one of London's most important pirate
❮ radio stations. After Give Up Art had completed their rebrand, packaging for CD releases was required. In order to keep costs down, Give Up Art shot portraits of each DJ, but in groups of three or four at one time, either around the management offices of the station or at club nights where the DJs would be playing. This left enough in the budget for each release to allow for a unique and personalized cover.

GIVE UP ART
UK

> This poster is proof of just how good DIY photography can be. With all photography done in-house, this really is a tour de force.

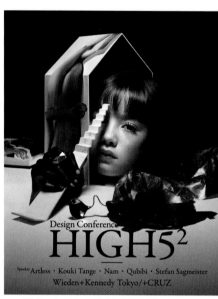

NAM – THE GRAPHIC COLLECTIVE
JAPAN

< The brief for this prospectus for CCW was to
∨ create a document that represents the identity of each of its three constituent art colleges: Camberwell College of Arts, Chelsea College of Art and Design, and Wimbledon College of Art. Ten students from each college were given a pack containing a disposable camera, a brief, and ten words to inspire them to produce the photography for the prospectuses. .

THIS IS STUDIO
UK

TIP

The differences between professional DSLRs and cheaper models is their build quality. Professional DSLRs are built to withstand the heavier use and abuse of life out on the road. Price varies greatly. Do you really need all the features a very expensive camera will give you, or is this best left to the professional?

> This campaign promoting safe driving consisted of posters and fliers. With limited budgets, the designers visualized their concepts by shooting friends in their own cars. They used a 3D modeler to create the robotic hand, which was then added in-house with Photoshop.

STEFANO MACCARELLI
ITALY

CASE STUDY:
TRAFFIC

The Scottish Artists Union (SAU) was a small, little-known, nonprofit organization with 100 members, but with a lot to offer anyone who joined, and a drive to quadruple membership within six months.

Traffic Design Consultants undertook all works at cost. A range of literature was required and, with no funds available, Scott Witham, Creative Director for Traffic, spent a day with SAU members to photograph their works, their studios, and themselves. This built up a pool of photography that would work across all new literature, posters, and promotional material. Within six months of releasing the new promotional material, they had achieved their goal.

TRAFFIC DESIGN CONSULTANTS
UK

STUDIO PHOTOGRAPHY

If you own a good-quality DSLR camera, or have access to one, put it to the best use, and as often as possible. You can save a lot of money by shooting your own images to include in design work, or as product shots of your own work.

This could be anything from photographing a brochure to update your website to shooting small commercial objects on behalf of a client. It should be possible to charge your client for doing this, but we would advise telling them that you are planning to take these shots in-house, and pitching your costs at about half what a professional photographer would charge. You will make money and have complete control over the shoot, and your client's budget will go further. This is very much a judgment call. If you are looking at taking a shot of a product for low-resolution web work and for product brochures, the home/office studio could be the best way to go; if you are looking at a product shot that will form the main part of a costly and national advertising campaign, we would advise leaving it to the professionals.

First and foremost, you will need a DSLR camera, a tripod, and a standard "all-purpose" lens as well as a good macro lens for close-ups. Try starting with a flat white or gray backdrop. Try to keep your background seamless. Large, inexpensive rolls of paper can be held up by a support system of rods and crossbars. Simple clamps can be used for keeping the backdrop from unrolling, and for weighing it down on the floor. It's best not to overpower your subject matter so, initially, stick to white, gray, or black backdrops. Bring in your lighting, but keep it simple and multidirectional.

Photographers would recommend a monolight with a strobe flash unit— a 150 watt/second monolight or stronger will suffice. For larger subjects we would suggest placing a small softbox over the monolight; this will diffuse the light and create a less harsh lighting environment. You can use a sync cord to connect your camera to the monolight, or a wireless flash control. For smaller items we would suggest creating a similar mini studio, but on a tabletop. You could even build your own softbox and place the objects to be photographed inside.

Remember, you can add lights as you see fit. Extra lights can be positioned and angled to eliminate any strong shadows.

Build your mini studio well away from a door or an area that sees a lot of traffic— you don't want someone tripping on cables and bringing everything crashing down. A corner of the boardroom is the perfect place. Setting up next to a window allows you to take advantage of natural light. Create enough space for your object to be at least half a meter (c. 20in) from the backdrop in order to prevent shadows. Your camera and softbox should be about the same distance from your subject.

Always take test images and adjust your aperture settings to suit. If you aren't familiar with camera settings, you can set your camera to automatic; if you really know your stuff, use a handheld light meter to test your lights and go by its recommended settings.

For speed and accuracy you can tether your photo booth to your computer or laptop. Each photo will then pop up instantly on your monitor, allowing you to make your color corrections immediately and save directly to your hard drive, thus removing the need for memory cards.

While most designers will simply work direct to Adobe Photoshop, programs such as Adobe Lightroom and Aperture can be used directly with your camera's proprietary software when shooting tethered. Most cameras should be set to Picture Transfer Protocol (PTP) and connected to your computer via USB or Firewire, but check your camera's settings.

These are the four basic steps for in-house photography:

1. Make sure your mini studio or softbox is maneuverable. The chances are you simply won't have the space to make this a permanent feature of your office or home, so you will need to store it somewhere, and keep it safe from damage.

2. Don't try to shoot objects that are too big to fit into your studio. The results will not be good enough and your client may feel let down. Keep your ambitions realistic; start small and work your way up. Most clients will manufacture small-scale objects that fit onto your tabletop. For larger objects such as furniture, cars, or people, we recommend leaving the shoot to professionals.

3. Lighting is almost as important as the camera itself. Even budget cameras will do a surprisingly good job if you get the lighting right.

4. From the very first shot you take in your studio, keep a record of how you took it—especially your perfect shots. Note the distance of the object from the backdrop, the position and number of lights, how much diffusion there was, and what camera settings and speeds you used. This information will be invaluable when you have to take a similar shot in the future.

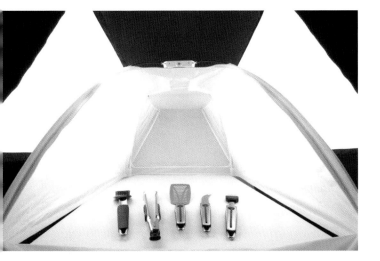

^ A good prime lens is a must; a softbox
‹ is a good investment if you plan on any amount of in-house photography.

ROYALTY-FREE PHOTOGRAPHY

NAIMA ALMEIDA
BRAZIL

The use of royalty-free imagery within the design scene has exploded over the past few years as imagery of a very high standard has become cheap and easy to download.

In years gone by it was a ludicrously overpriced and complex process to order a stock shot. Quite often you also had to pay extra, depending on who the client was, if a reprint was requested; or you had to purchase shots you didn't need simply to get the one you did. With the advent of broadband and the ability to download high-resolution shots, all of this changed, and for the better.

Some shots are free to download, others require that you block-buy credits and use these (within a set timescale) as

and when required. Either way, it is very important that you check the terms and conditions of use of each site before you download and use a shot. Always be a little suspicious of something that is free, and always check the terms that apply to each individual download.

The downside of stock photography is that the shot will not be exclusive to you—it may well have been used hundreds of times already.

With sites such as www.flickr.com, which offer free downloadable photographs, you do need to check each individual shot for copyright permissions. Some photographers won't grant copyright permission; others simply require a credit in the publication.

^ For this album artwork the CD itself was printed onto SMD (semi-metallic discs), a new medium that reduces the production cost by 80%. The cover artwork was created using a mix of royalty-free photography, old studio photos, and photos from the band itself. The fonts were picked from an old catalog, scanned, and recreated to compose the words.

Online image libraries

www.123rf.com
www.acclaimimages.com
www.alamy.com
www.bigstockphoto.com
www.canstockphoto.com
www.cepolina.com
www.corbis.com
www.crestock.com
www.dreamstime.com
www.easystockphotos.com
www.en.fotolia.com
www.everystockphoto.com
www.fotosearch.co.uk
www.freedigitalphotos.net
www.freefoto.com
www.freeimages.co.uk
www.freemediagoo.com
www.freephotosbank.com
www.freepixels.com
www.freerangestock.com
www.freestockphotos.com
www.gettyimages.com
www.imageafter.com
www.inmagine.com
www.istockphoto.com
www.jupiterimages.co.uk
www.morguefile.com
www.openphoto.net
www.photogen.com
www.photorack.net
www.photos.com
www.photospin.com
www.pixmac.com
www.public-domain-photos.com
www.punchstock.co.uk
www.shutterstock.com
www.stockphotoasia.com
www.stockvault.net
www.stockxpert.com
www.sxc.hu
www.texturewarehouse.com
www.unprofound.com

❯ All imagery for these posters was sourced
and downloaded from low-cost image banks,
brought together in Adobe Photoshop, cut
down by hand, and finished in-house.

GRAPHIC DIVERSION
BELGIUM

CASE STUDY:
SOCIO DESIGN

The worldwide property investment company Seven Continent Investment (7CI) commissioned Socio to create a brochure to promote their services.

The brochure features double-page-spread panoramic photographs sourced online from royalty-free sites. The shots were digitally enhanced to increase their vibrancy and printed on uncoated stock with an overall sealer varnish in line with the smart, high-end image associated with the 7CI brand. With strong use of color, beautiful typography, and a keen choice of stock photography, Socio created an effective, successful brochure.

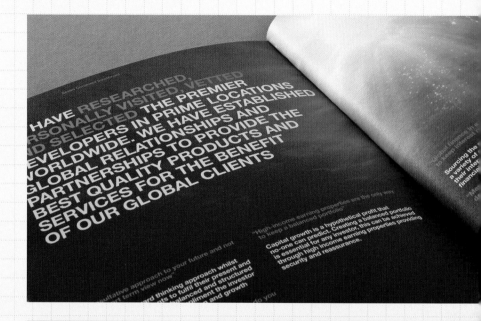

SOCIO DESIGN
UK

FLÁVIO HOBO
PORTUGAL

‹ Lisbon-based designer Flávio Hobo created this poster to promote an electro-acoustic and percussion concert. To keep costs down, Hobo chose to buy just one royalty-free photo, and edited it in Photoshop to represent speakers. To get an image of the vibes' keys to use in the shot, Hobo hired a photographer—as this is a not a common instrument, suitable images weren't available on stock sites. Often, the best way to use royalty-free shots is to mix them with your own rather than relying on them entirely.

⌄ This project consisted of fliers and posters. The stock images came from subscription service Jupiter Images and were adjusted and combined in Photoshop.

ERIK BORRESON
USA

Traffic Design Consultants were commissioned to produce a brochure for friend and collaborator Martyn Robertson; they had recently worked together to create the brand identity for his new venture Urbancroft, a digital film and video production company. Working closely with the client and agreeing on styles, Traffic downloaded a large number of royalty-free shots and mixed these with shots suppled by Robertson to create a series of artistic photomontages. These were used throughout the brochure and on the website, saving further on both time and funds.

TRAFFIC DESIGN CONSULTANTS
UK

POULIN + MORRIS
USA

∧ Stock photography can be used in many different ways. With this book cover, Poulin + Morris overlaid various images to get the desired effect.

‹ To keep costs down, Lionel Scholtes purchased the shots he needed from www.stockxpert.com. With a cheap daily subscription rate, he could download up to 25 high-res shots a day.

GRAPHIC DIVERSION
BELGIUM

This pocket calendar features photographic illustrations designed in-house by PARAGON Marketing Communications. These depict the personality of the company. PARAGON used stock photography and printed all artwork on one single sheet. The calendars were then die-cut from this sheet—a much cheaper option than printing them separately.

PARAGON MARKETING COMMUNICATIONS
KUWAIT

Tokyo-based Sunday Project creates all the visual works for free graphic design magazine *Sketch*. They treat downloaded shots graphically, using various processes, including halftone dot screens, etc. Keeping the costs down in this way allows for larger print runs and at the same time captures the cheap, lively feel that marks free-magazine design.

Sketch

sundayproject.jp

Sketch

Silence

Claire Orrell created the artwork for punk band The Twisted Minds. Following a discussion with the band, Orrell felt that photo collage would best represent the anarchic and politically charged nature of its music. She downloaded free imagery and mixed this with shots of the band and shots she took herself. All images were manipulated in Photoshop.

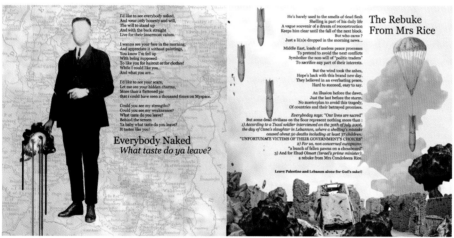

Peter Eekelaert used a royalty-free shot and layered it with his own 3D renders for this poster.

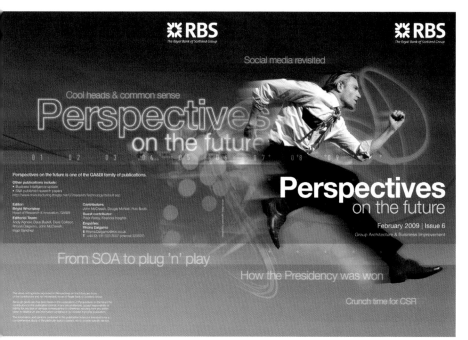

Traffic Design Consultants produces *Perspectives Magazine* quarterly for the Royal Bank of Scotland Group. To ensure the magazine's survival, costs must be kept to a minimum and are regularly scrutinized. For speed, a set grid was established, and all inner spreads rely heavily on royalty-free photography. The self-set brief is that no purchased stock shot can be used without heavy manipulation. This stops any imagery in the magazine being criticized for simply being downloaded. Images are often several shots merged together and the cover often involves up to 20 separate shots used together.

INSPIRATION:
BLOGS & FORUMS

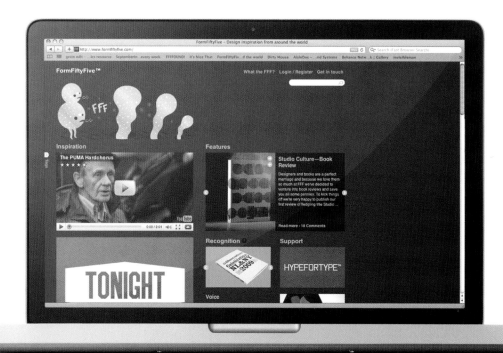

With graphic design, for which communication is mostly visual, the rise in the popularity of blogs has been phenomenal. A blog (simply a contraction of the term "web log") is a website, usually maintained by an individual, with very regular entries of text or other material, including graphics or video.

Many design-focused blogs provide commentary or news on a particular subject; others become online diaries as a project or event grows. A typical blog combines text, images, and links to other blogs, web pages, and media related to its topic. Readers (bloggers) are able to leave comments, allowing debate and online conversation to flourish. All blogs are primarily textual, but many focus on art, videos, photographs, or music.

Blogs are far more than simply online magazines. They are an honest and instant window into the creative world where conversations and debate can flourish and grow. Creative blogs have allowed a new generation of designer to develop a voice that will always have an audience. This is where you will find the latest word on design.

^ Blogs are generally free, usually unedited or censored, and often hold up-to-the-minute conversations, both visually and in text.

The following list is just an inroad. Many of these blogs have their own set of lists and links to a wealth of other blogs, journals, studios, and online tools for designers. Hopping from blog to blog, you may see an element of repetition, but a new, fresh conversation will always be taking place.

Every designer will have a bank of their favorite online sources tuned to their tastes and sources of inspiration. Sites such as FFFFOUND and Dropular are simply banks of imagery found from other online sources. These kinds of blogs can provide a fantastic way to sift through quick hits of inspiration. Others act more as journals or online magazines, with in-depth articles, interviews, and links to the latest handy online sources, free fonts, and imagery. Some even have forums and extensive user-based comments sections where discussions about the latest big-name rebrand or plagiarism can get really heated.

One of the most obvious advantages of keeping up with blogs is that you can use them as a platform to showcase your work. Studios that update their websites often announce events and new work on some of the most popular and renowned blogs, such as Formfiftyfive, Dirtymouse, and Aisleone.

BLOGS / JOURNALS

www.acejet170.typepad.com
www.aisleone.net
www.bibliodyssey.blogspot.com
www.bitique.co.uk
www.booooooom.com
www.cpluv.com
www.designobserver.com
www.dezeen.com
www.dirtymouse.com
www.fleuron.com
www.formfiftyfive.com
www.fubiz.net
www.grafikcache.com
www.grainedit.com
www.graphichug.com
www.heavyeyes.net
www.hipyoungthing.com
www.itsnicethat.com
www.manystuff.org
www.modernthought.co.uk
www.nolegacy.com
www.original-linkage.blogspot.com
www.reformrevolution.com
www.septemberindustry.co.uk
www.somuchpileup.blogspot.com
www.swisslegacy.com
www.thegridsystem.org
www.the-refined.com
www.thestrangeattractor.net
www.typojungle.net
www.welcometohr.com

COLLATED IMAGERY / INSPIRATION

www.buamai.com
www.butdoesitfloat.com
www.creativeoutput.net/blog
www.dropular.net
www.ffffound.com
www.flickr.com
www.yayeveryday.com
www.ypeish.com

PACKAGE DESIGN BLOG

www.lovelypackage.com
www.thedieline.com

IDENTITY BLOG

www.underconsideration.com/brandnew

CHAPTER 4: MATERIALS & FINISHING

ENDANGERED SPECIES

SPECIES IN DANGER OF EXTINCTION THROUGHOUT OR A SIGNIFICANT PART OF ITS RANGE

ΕΙΔΗ ΥΠΟ ΕΞΑΦΑΝΙΣΗ

FORMS & FOLDS

❤ staynice created this poster a little like a jigsaw puzzle. It is composed of 16 separate areas, all of the same size, each one with its own unique design created from multiples of the same image. The poster also had mulitiple uses: cross-folded down, it was used as an invitation and a teaser campaign.

STAYNICE
THE NETHERLANDS

Not every piece of design needs to be a standard size, portrait, and stitched or stapled down the spine. It's more than likely that as soon as you move away from standard finishes and folding, the printing costs will increase. Pages folding out, gatefold center-page spreads, oversized paper, and cross-folding will all add to the cost. Or will they?

They will only cost more if the printer delivers the print fully finished to your specifications. It is often possible to instruct the printer to supply the job bound and scored, but flat (i.e., unfolded). If the additional cost is due to finishing, look into the possibilities of folding yourself, by hand. Can additional dust jackets be supplied separately and fitted in-house? If you want to add stickers or wraparound ties, ensure you do these yourself. It can be time-consuming, but it does save money in the long run. Limit yourself to a fixed number; do you really have time to hand finish 1,000 brochures? Even 500 will take quite a bit of time. Alternatively, rope in some help. If this is saving the client money, will they provide a body or two to help? The best time for hand finishing is usually out of office hours; assemble a team, get pizza in, put on some good music, and you'll be surprised just how much fun hand-folding 1,000 annual reports can actually become.

It's important that you weigh up the cost saving against the length of time required to complete the finishing. Remember, a unique hand-finished piece of work will always feel that little bit more special and make a fantastic addition to your portfolio.

Proekt decided to create this brochure—for Parad Fashion Boutique—as a pack of cards, which reduced costs by eliminating the need for binding. With Parad's new range taking its inspiration from space travel, Proekt gave the pack a space-age feel.

TIP

Many design studios offer work-experience placements to final-year design students. These usually last two weeks. Don't bring in students simply to do all your hand finishing and folding, but to ask a student to spend a single day helping with building or finishing a piece of design work is totally acceptable. It also helps the student understand that designing does not always mean sitting in front of a computer pushing a mouse about. The hand finishing and construction approach is still very much in demand.

PROEKT
RUSSIA

DC WORKS
THE NETHERLANDS

‹ These cards were designed for a company concerned with making the clubscene more aware of sustainability. By perforating the business card, you are able to split it in two and give it a away for a second time.

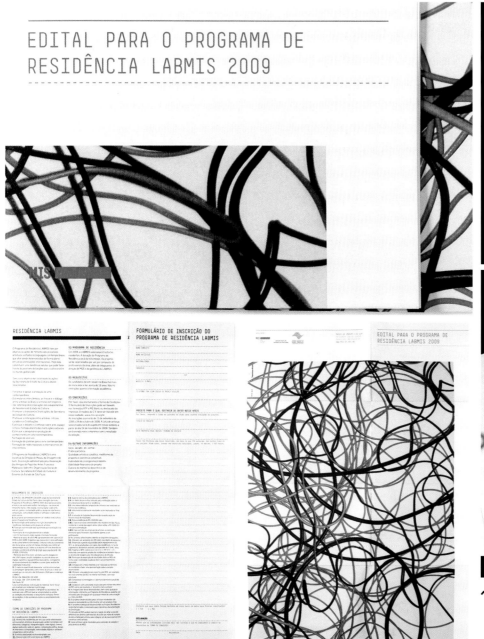

PS.2 ARQUITETURA + DESIGN
BRAZIL

REMAKE
USA

^ A new visual identity for the Museum of Image and Sound in São Paulo. It was imperative that all future printed literature for the museum be cost-effective. The solution was to use small formats for catalogs, invitations, and folders, and to produce many of the works in single spot colors. The color and unusual folding are two simple elements employed to solve the problems of cost versus creativity.

^ Remake created literature to promote Teague's presence at an aviation tradeshow in Hamburg. To minimize costs and maximize impact, they developed a large-scale broadsheet format. The job was printed cold web and came off the press folded and booked, requiring only a trim. The design capitalized on the newsprint substrate and one-color print (black).

CASE STUDY: ZYNC

Zync developed an annual report for Casey House, a hospital providing exemplary treatment for people affected by HIV/AIDS. The brief was to celebrate the partnerships vital to the success of Casey House. Through the theme "together we can," portraits of real supporters printed in an extreme landscape format illustrated the support for Casey House.

With the report being 80½in (c. 2m) long, there were very few options for print production that would be cost-effective. Working closely with the printer, Zync decided to print the report in three separate sections. The diagram illustrates the production options used. Once printed, the press sheets were die-cut, creased, and folded. The folded sections were then sent to the bookbinders where they were tipped together by hand. The creasing and cutting dies were modified twice prior to production to ensure an exact fit during tipping because once the pieces were creased and folded, the bookbinders would have little opportunity to fix any alignment issues.

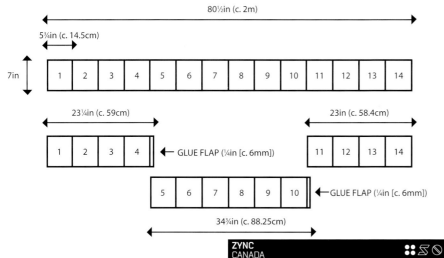

80½in (c. 2m)

5¾in (c. 14.5cm)

7in

| 1 | 2 | 3 | 4 | 5 | 6 | 7 | 8 | 9 | 10 | 11 | 12 | 13 | 14 |

23¼in (c. 59cm)   23in (c. 58.4cm)

| 1 | 2 | 3 | 4 | ← GLUE FLAP (¼in [c. 6mm]) | 11 | 12 | 13 | 14 |

| 5 | 6 | 7 | 8 | 9 | 10 | ← GLUE FLAP (¼in [c. 6mm])

34¾in (c. 88.25cm)

ZYNC
CANADA

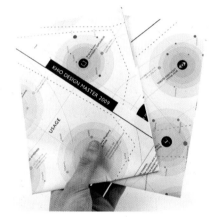

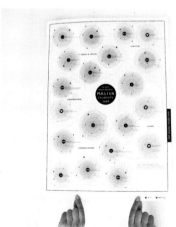

herneheim.

⌄ Peter Herneheim is a Stockholm-based music photographer. The aim for his graphic identity was to help establish him as a professional music photographer and make it possible for him to get unique access to the contemporary music scene. The guitar pick is a central part of the identity, acting as both logo and business card. No more expensive than printing a regular business card, it proved a lot more effective.

ONE SIZE FITS ALL
SWEDEN

⟨ This literature for the Oslo National Academy of the Arts was made so that it could be folded in two different ways: to work as a pamphlet or a poster. To keep costs down, all folding was done by hand.

MAX SCHRØDER
NORWAY

To keep costs down, the cover of REG's brochure for Peter Bond was printed in one spot color. Text pages were printed onto extra-thin, uncoated paper and the color image pages were printed in full color onto thin gloss paper. The whole folding mechanism of the brochure allows the inner pages to fold in and the cover to form an envelope, thus avoiding further packaging costs.

REG
UK

São Paulo–based Nu Design had a very low budget to produce this CD packaging, but wanted to avoid the regular-issue acrylic CD box. The standard acrylic pack is very cheap, so Nu Design knew it would be very difficult to come in cheaper and had to convince the client they could do it and still deliver a highly attractive piece of packaging. It created a single piece of design that could be printed and cut from sheets of cheaply produced 300gsm Kraft paper. Sticking to a single spot black, and hand folding and gluing each pack, ensured that all was achieved with great success.

TÓ BRANDILEONE

NU DESIGN
BRAZIL

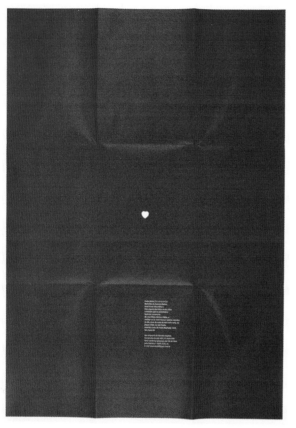

ps.2 arquitetura + design created this wedding invitation for designers Fábio Prata and Flávia Nalon. The studio chose to translate the concept of love in the form of a single color—red. Through multiple folding, the red, at first, is only visible through a small die-cut heart. It's not until the massive sheet is folded out that all is revealed. Costs were also kept down by printing onto a thin, cost-effective, uncoated paper.

PS.2 ARQUITETURA + DESIGN
BRAZIL

This document uses a Z-fold to cunning effect in this book of four short stories by Kevin Boniface. Each side uses a different single color to distinguish the sections.

MUSIC
UK

‹ Centro is a design, film, and product design university located in Mexico City.
⌄ The identity had to be simple, yet visually enticing. Blok's aim was to design a smart and effective series of posters printed on economical bond paper and with a brochure printed on the other side. Blok also ensured that the printer's make-ready's were not thrown away, but collected these and transformed them into envelopes for later use. The result was random imagery that appeared throughout the stationery.

BLOK
BRAZIL

> This design provides an invitation, catalog, and poster all in one. The poster folds twice to become the catalog, and three times to become the invitation—a clever and cost-effective way of producing three pieces of literature from a single piece of printing.

ALEXANDER EGGER
AUSTRIA

> For this promotional giveaway for the 2325 club in Stavanger, Norway, a single piece of print was produced for use both as a poster and the CD packaging itself.

AL DENTE
NORWAY

ALOOF
UK

‹ The brief was to rebrand and reposition a small organic bakery to enable them to compete on a national level. The innovative pack opens flat to create a cutting and serving surface; is manufactured locally, using a minimum of print and production processes; requires no glue; and is 100% recyclable.

› This promotional mailer folds out to a small poster size. Each sheet was die-cut, and the trimmed area was used to form a separate mini-print. Printing the illustrations in black allowed the use of three extra Pantone inks, creating an interesting color palette. The mailers and prints, limited to a run of 500, were all signed by the artist.

SIX
UK

STUDIO ASTRID STAVRO
SPAIN

❮ For this catalog accompanying an exhibition
❮ of the international translations of Catalan
novelist Mercé Rodoreda, Studio Astrid Stavro
devised a folding case to avoid the high binding
costs otherwise required. The catalog itself
was designed as a series of 11 postcards, each
featuring a different-language translation.

BIZ–R
UK

❮ For this brief, biz-R maximized sheet usage to
ensure lower print costs. These print savings
allowed for a more creative finish—a roll-back
cover. A mix of recycled paper, silk, and
uncoated stocks was used.

The theme of this festival was, simply, "No budget available; make your own festival," which led THIS IS Studio to follow a DIY aesthetic, based on wallpaper. They created programs, a website, and screenprinted posters. All folding and rolling was done by hand to keep costs to a minimum.

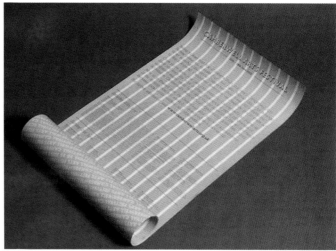

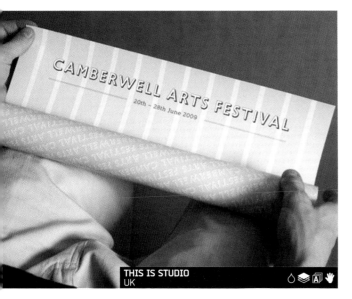

THIS IS STUDIO
UK

KVORNING DESIGN & KOMMUNIKATION
DENMARK

For the Danish stand at the 2008 Womex World Music Expo, a poster and a brochure listing the Danish exhibitors were required. To reduce printing costs, Kvorning designed the brochure in the form of a poster, which could be roll-folded for easy handling.

PAPER STOCKS

Choosing the paper can be one of the most important decisions you make for a piece of printed design, not only from a cost, but also from a quality point of view.

It can be a real challenge as there are so many things to take into consideration, for example, ink lift, weight, finish, and, of course, financial outlay. Different papers can create different color tones when printing. Even if you use exactly the same artwork as a previous job, the paper can affect the way it looks and feels. Ink sits on top of coated papers (silk, gloss, and matte), but sinks into uncoated papers (offset), resulting in a duller color. Today there is a huge range of papers available, and it is worth having a little knowledge about them so that you can make an informed decision as to what will work best for your budget. Following is a list of the most common types of paper, along with their benefits and drawbacks.

Gloss-Coated

Gloss papers are usually coated in china clay to give them a high shine and smooth appearance. One benefit of using a gloss-coated paper is that the ink lift is excellent, which gives great definition to illustrations and photography and makes flat color very vibrant. Another is that it dries very well and is unlikely to need a sealer to prevent it rubbing off. There are, however, some drawbacks to using a gloss: it is sometimes prone to cracking when it is folded, and it can also be prone to marking due to its high shine.

TIP

Talk to your print and paper suppliers—they have a great knowledge of stocks, weights, ink lifts, and how much each element will add to the job. It doesn't cost anything to get their advice and they can help you come up with a good, cost-effective solution. Be honest with them about your budget and be clear about what you expect to achieve. Use their expertise and knowledge to your advantage.

Silk-Coated

Silk-coated papers sit somewhere between uncoated and gloss papers and can be a good compromise. A silk has a lower surface shine than a gloss and a less textured finish than a matte. You will still get a good ink lift from a silk, but the colors will not be as vibrant as on a gloss. Inks do not dry or harden as well on a silk as on a gloss and therefore require a sealer varnish, which will add slightly to the print costs.

Matte-Coated

Matte-coated papers have a clay coating that gives them a smooth, dull finish; they have a slightly textured feel and no surface shine. Images will not have quite such a good ink lift as on a gloss or a silk paper; however, this can often add to the overall feel of the print. Inks take longer to dry on matte-coated stocks, so a sealer varnish, a relatively inexpensive finish, is recommended in order to prevent rub-off.

These posters feature duotone images printed onto uncoated newsprint stock. For the top poster, type was overprinted in red, and for sthe bottom poster, the type was foil-stamped.

DUCKIE BROWN SPRING/SUMMER 2007
THE ATELIER
BRYANT PARK TENTS, NEW YORK CITY
(ENTRANCE ON 6TH AVENUE AT 41ST STREET)
SEPTEMBER 8, 2006
6:00 PM
RSVP: WILLIAMSON PR 212.206.5307 EMILY@WILLIAMSONPR.COM

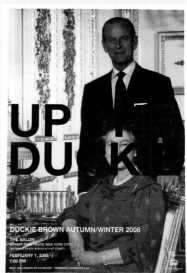

DUCKIE BROWN AUTUMN/WINTER 2008
THE SALON
BRYANT PARK TENTS, NEW YORK CITY
(ENTRANCE ON 6TH AVENUE AT 41ST STREET)
FEBRUARY 1, 2008
1:00 PM
RSVP: WILLIAMSON PR 212.206.5307 PRESS@WILLIAMSONPR.COM

SUBTITLE
ITALY

This annual report was printed on large-format newsprint, giving it a broadsheet supplement look and feel. The benefits were numerous: the recycled newsprint suited the client's values, there was more space for content, and it was relatively cheap to print.

THE BIG PICTURE
UK

This invitation to the Manchester School of Art degree show was printed onto translucent paper to allow showthrough of print from the reverse side.

ADAM MORRIS
UK

TIP

Remember to take time at the start of your project to go through your paper options and discuss this with your clients. Find out what sort of paper they are expecting and what they are willing to pay for. Choosing the correct weight and finish could save you money. If you are specifying an uncoated paper, show your client a sample to make sure they understand that the finished job will not be glossy.

Recycled

Recycled papers have become more popular in recent times due to their environmental credentials.

Uncoated

Uncoated paper is also known as offset paper. Typically, it has a more textured feeling than any of the coated stocks and this can be used for deliberate effects in a print project. The ink lift is not as strong as on any of the coated papers; more of the ink soaks in, which means images will not appear as defined as when printed on a coated stock. This also means that jobs can take longer to dry, which should be taken into account in scheduling.

Homemade

You can, for very short-run projects, make your own paper. This can be a fun and cost-effective way to create a unique look and feel for your job. It is unlikely that you will be able to supply homemade paper for a printer to use, but you can screen-print or rubber-stamp onto it.

Almost all the large paper companies have swatch books of the papers in their range. These are a very useful thing to have in your design studio as they have examples of different print finishes and different weights to let you see how the paper handles. These swatch books (supplied free by the paper manufacturers) usually contain useful technical information

TIP

Most papers over 170gsm will need to be scored prior to folding. This adds to the finishing costs of a job as it is a separate process; on a large print run it can add a significant amount to the final bill. If you are printing a simple, folded promotional flier, does it need to be on thick card? Can you run it on 150gsm stock and save money?

about the paper—for example, whether it is laser safe, FSC accredited, etc. Your paper company can also give you a good idea of where the stock is placed price-wise and what it is most commonly used for, i.e., for stationery, brochures, etc. This will help you see what other people use it for and is a good indicator of a reliable, affordable product. Some paper companies and printers will have samples of printed jobs to show you the quality achievable, and will be able to tell you what that job cost to produce. Seeing a sample can often help you weigh up quality of finish against cost.

Paper Weights

The density of all types of paper and paperboard is expressed in terms of grams per square meter (gsm). Typical office paper is 80gsm, which is quite an affordable, versatile weight. The heavier the paper, the fewer your printing options, and the greater the printing costs.

> Music were commissioned by Manchester Enterprises to produce six reports, each containing a wealth of information, but to a limited budget. To bring life to the reports, Music produced them all on special sugar paper using simple spot-color graphics.

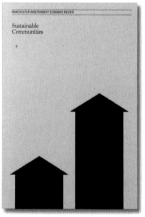

MUSIC
UK

Paper weight is a very important element in a design job and careful selection of weights can save you money. If a job doesn't have many pages, it can be beneficial if you spec the whole job on the same weight and incorporate a self cover in the design.

Postal costs should be taken into consideration; if the client is sending out a brochure, they will be charged according to the weight of the package.

Paper weight can also play a part in the finishing of a job. As a general rule, papers under 170gsm don't need to be scored before folding. This isn't always true, and the printer should always be consulted, but it is worth remembering that certain finishing problems can be avoided if you choose the right paper in the right weight.

TIP

Most paper manufacturers run a sample service, which often includes making blank dummies. This is usually free and is a fantastic way to get paper samples made up into your proposed format and over to the client for approval. This is for minimal quantities only—paper companies will soon know if you request too many to simply be samples.

TIP

Is it really necessary to specify a make of paper for every job? Does a review document that has no pictures, but is purely a legally binding factual piece, really require a named brand of paper? Pick what type of stock you want (offset, silk, or gloss) and ask your printer to quote for this using their "house" papers. Quite often a printer will have secured a deal with a large paper manufacturer to buy in large quantities of high-quality silks, glosses, etc. Go with these and you can keep the costs down.

❤ Sour, an urban clothing store in Belgium, tasked Nit'ras with producing promotional literature with a difference. Nit'ras chose a fully recycled paper because of its strong grain and lumpy texture, which they used to bring the subtle gray print to life.

NIT'RAS
BELGIUM

RECYCLED PAPER

˅ Artiva Design wanted a 100% recycled stock for their self-promotional posters. Printing was in single spot black, and with cross-folding, the posters doubled up as a flexible-format magazine.

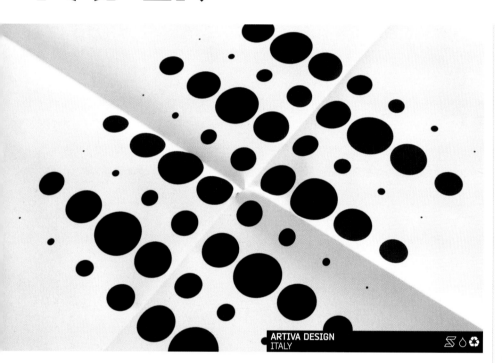

ARTIVA DESIGN
ITALY

Environmental concerns are moving closer to the top of company agendas and are having an increasing influence on the materials selected for use in their products. Graphic design is no different, but of equal concern is cost.

The choice of papers today is vast. There are papers made from virgin fibers and recycled papers, and textured and colored ranges of varying stocks and weights, offering a solution for every possible need.

Recycled paper shouldn't cost the earth (excuse the pun). The paper industry is facing up to its responsibilities by making recycled products more affordable and creating bigger ranges with different levels of recycled content. As the increase in demand has brought the costs tumbling, recycled and conventional paper prices are finally evening out. The refinement of the papermaking process and the significant reduction in the levels of energy and water needed to make recycled paper compared with conventional paper has helped to close the price gap.

To improve the quality of recycled papers, some paper mills include a certain amount of virgin fiber. These papers usually carry a label showing the percentage of recycled content—25%, 50%, or 75%—and this will affect the price of the paper. In the past, virgin fiber was very cheap, so recycled papers often cost more, but the situation is changing. Don't be afraid to ask your printer to compare the costs of a recycled and nonrecycled paper stock; you may be pleasantly surprised.

The decision to use recycled paper is down to personal or company attitudes to corporate social responsibility (CSR). It is down to the design team and the client to work together to make a judgment for each project as regards the balance of the environmental impact versus the cost. A compromise can always be found through choice of paper, printer, etc. As with all cost-cutting exercises, every avenue should be explored in order to get the best solution for the best price.

This recyclable packaging for the reissue of two "twentieth-century classics" from iconic British designers Robin and Lucienne Day used recycled materials and a minimum number of print and production processes (one-color screenprint and one die-cut). The construction, using no glue fastenings, reflects the Days' approach to design.

CERTIFIED PAPERS

There are many paper certifications, one of the most widely recognized of which is FSC (Forest Stewardship Council). The FSC is an independent, nonprofit organization established to promote the responsible management of the world's forests. FSC-certified papers are an eco alternative to recycled papers.

The certification signifies that both the printer and the designer actively support sound environmental practices. In order to use the FSC logo, the product must have flowed through the FSC chain of custody from the FSC-certified forest, to a paper manufacturer or merchant, and finally to a printer who has FSC certification.

FACTS

> Less than 40% of the pulp needed to make the paper we consume is recoverable.

> Making quality/white paper from recycled fiber (upcycling) is more expensive than making regular or certified paper.

> Most papers available today are certified to some level, i.e., they contain at least some recycled fibers, or are FSC-certified.

> There are only a few truly 100% recycled papers available. If you want this, make sure the paper you select carries either the FSC100 logo or an equivalent certified branding.

Tricorne tray
designed by Robin Day

Pure linen teatowel
designed by Lucienne Day

ALOOF
UK

> Osuna Nursery asked 3 Advertising to develop a box tray to hold plants. The recycled material lent itself well to the message printed on it.

∨ Naughtyfish created this poster for a design exhibition. The first poster was sent out as a call for entries, then the black plate was overprinted to create a second publicity poster.

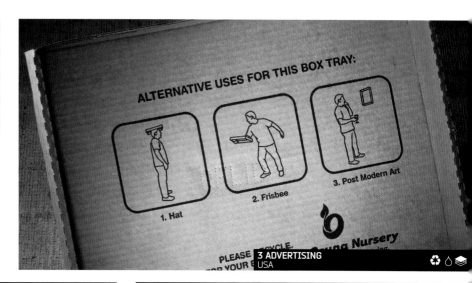

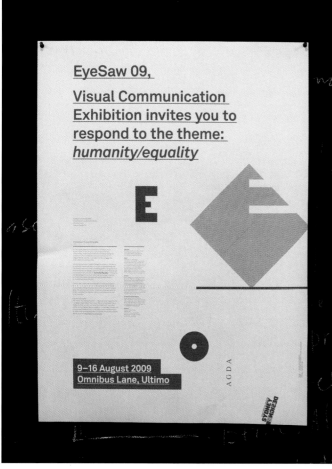

BOCA
BRAZIL

◁ Marcos Boca Ceravolo created a typographic poster using the expression "Express Yourself Before You Wreck Yourself." He wanted to do something analog and tactile, and to reuse things that were sitting in his studio, including a stack of old business cards. He cut the letters from these business cards, arranged them on his cutting mat, and photographed them.

TIP

When using an FSC-certified paper, it is important that you also use an FSC-accredited printer; if the printer isn't certified, you won't be able to use the FSC logo.

▶ Penelope is a successful photographer so her identity had to be unique and aesthetically stylish. Furthermore, an environmental solution was requested. To achieve this, a thick recycled cardboard was used for her business card and printed ink-free by debossing the paper. Three colors of paper were used, all sourced from remaining material left over from a previous project. The photographer's logo was then printed on a round sticker and was glued to the back of the card. The same sticker was also used on the letterheads and the envelopes in order to avoid further cost and ink-based production.

KANELLA
GREECE

FINISHES

Although conventional litho printing is the cheapest form of production for larger runs, there are many finishes that can help a piece stand out.

One very popular finish is spot UV (ultraviolet) varnishing. UV varnishing gives a slick, glossy coating that makes the finished printing appear richer and more luxurious.

With foil blocking, foil is applied to the paper using a heated metal die, and the design of the die is stamped onto the foil and paper. Foils are available in a range of colors, but gold and silver are the most common.

Through embossing, a raised design or pattern can be stamped into paper or card. Debossing will produce a recessed rather than a raised pattern.

Thermography applies heat to powder and ink to give a high-gloss, raised image. Rarely used, this gives an almost plastic feel to the raised print.

Matte lamination applies a very thin, dull, clear plastic sheeting to a printed document; gloss lamination applies a shiny sheeting. Laminating enhances the appearance of printed images and provides protection for your documents, helping to prevent tearing and creasing.

These are just a few of the print finishes available. They all add to the cost of a job, but what if they were used instead of printing? Can they save money and look as good on their own? Yes, but only if used wisely. If you are creating a simple printed piece that requires standout, any of these finishes could be used instead of conventional printing. Only the lamination would need an additional print finish.

ALEXANDER EGGER
AUSTRIA

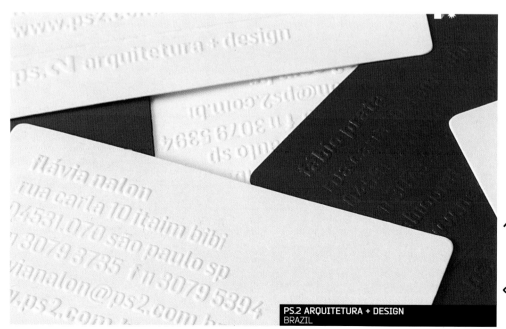

PS.2 ARQUITETURA + DESIGN
BRAZIL

▲ For this corporate identity for an Austrian carpenter, a wooden stamp of the logo marque was created so that it could be applied to all communication materials, giving a personal and individual touch

‹ ps.2 produced its business cards in plain card stocks of various colors, which made the most of the blind embossing they used in place of conventional ink printing.

> This beautifully produced single-spot-color brochure was supplied with sets of brightly colored kiss-cut stickers (in fluorescents and metallics), inviting recipients to add their own messages and flashes of color.

KIDNAP YOUR DESIGNER
BELGIUM

On its own, the laminate (a clear protective coating) would not convey any message. Invites, wedding stationery, certificates, business cards, brochure covers ... it is possible to save money on all of these by using a special finish instead of full color. Foil blocking and spot UV work particularly well on top of lamination; thermography and embossing/debossing work beautifully on plain white card.

> To achieve this effect, a spot-color stamp was overlaid on conventional litho printing.

CHRISTOF NARDIN
AUSTRIA

> Fabrice Praeger produced this New Year card, limited to a run of 700, by rubber-stamping onto paper handkerchiefs. The stamp reads "à vos souhaits!" (the French response to a sneeze), but a clever play on words means it also says "best wishes."

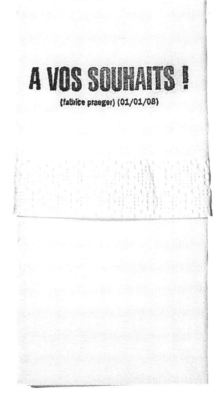

A VOS SOUHAITS !
(fabrice praeger) (01/01/08)

FABRICE PRAEGER
FRANCE

> Rough Fiction theater group required a visual identity that was highly flexible and economical. The solution was to create a set of rubber stamps. Endlessly reproducible onto any item, the stamp gives a sense of individuality and exclusivity, while removing the requirement for expensive print production.

RUBBER STAMPING

Rubber stamping is another handy and often overlooked technique that can be used to highlight small pieces of information, such as an image or a logo, saving both time and money on smaller print runs.

The basic rubber stamp is created by molding, laser cutting, or carving into a sheet of rubber. This can even be done by hand. The patterned rubber or plastic is then attached to a solid apparatus such as a block of wood or acrylic. Once coated with ink, the rubber stamp is ready to use. Rubber stamps are generally available in two varieties: a traditional handle-mount stamp or a self-inking stamp.

Handle-Mount Rubber Stamp
A handle-mount stamp consists of a rubber die attached to some form of handle, to be inked by hand after each impression. If your job doesn't require a lot of stamping, or you plan to use more than one color of ink, this sort of stamp is a very cost-effective alternative to a self-inking stamp.

Self-Inking Stamp
Self-inking stamps have a die affixed to a small moving device within the unit. The die comes into contact with an ink pad when depressed and then returns to be impressed on the item to be stamped. Because of this built-in ink pad, thousands of impressions can be made without manually reinking, making it the number one choice for speed.

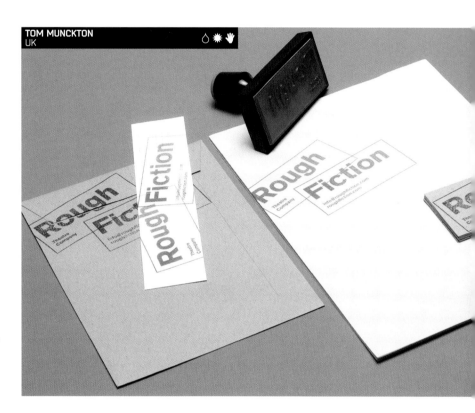

TOM MUNCKTON
UK

Rubber stamps are perfect for stamping all sorts of materials by hand where an otherwise unnecessary, but possibly expensive print run would be required. Large quantities of in-house stationery—business cards, letterheads, and promotional items—are popular choices for rubber stamping. Signing multiple business letters, cards, or screenprints, for example, can take a great deal of time and effort, depending on the quantity. Stamping eliminates this problem. This can also give the document the special feel of being a limited edition.

> The cost of this identity for environmentalist Robert Massengale was that of two rubber stamps and an ink pad. This stationery system instantly transforms any paper stock into a business card.

PS.2 ARQUITETURA + DESIGN
BRAZIL

^ This self-promotional gift was limited to 300
> copies. The kit contained a calendar, notepads,
pencils, and a collection of rubber stamps.
To create all this on a low budget, ps.2 sourced
all the material as cheaply as possible by buying
direct from the manufacturers and constructing
all the elements by hand in-house. Each kit was
stamped and numbered prior to sending out.

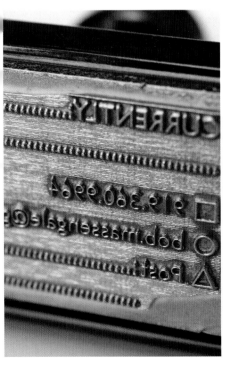

JOSHUA GAJOWNIK
USA

TIP

One-color stickers, using a single printed color as a background, but leaving the copy white-out, can make for a great, attractive, and effective image. Also, if the stickers are to be distributed as promo items, most printers can print on the disposable backing as well. Don't waste that space—use it to provide a related piece of information such as a web address or phone number.

SCALE TO FIT
THE NETHERLANDS

⌄ Printed on shiny metallic foil, these stickers make anything look good. They were applied to all forms of stationery, including letterheads, business cards, and compliments slips.

010 4760123.

WE COME IN PEACE   RESCALE@SCALETOFIT.COM

SCALE TO FIT   DELFTSEPLEIN 36ᶜ | 3013 AA ROTTERDAM | TEL: 010-476 0123 | FAX: 010-477 0525 | WWW.SCALETOFIT.COM |

010 4760123.

DENNIS VAN DER MEULE   06 288 32 532 | DENNIS@SCALETOFIT.COM

SCALE TO FIT   DELFTSEPLEIN 36ᶜ | 3013 AA ROTTERDAM | TEL: 010-476 0123 | FAX: 010-477 0525 | WWW.SCALETOFIT.COM |

STICKERS

Stickers have become highly effective marketing tools. They are also a simple, but very useful and cost-effective method of adding something extra to a document.

Where a small black-and-white print run needs a bit of color injected, a sticker is an excellent way to flag up a particular detail or piece of information, perhaps even to seal a document or envelope.

Stickers are also an extremely helpful way of getting the most use from a single print run. For example, you can save on the printing costs of posters for a monthly event or meeting by including only the basic details on the poster, and setting the time and date on a sticker, which can be updated each month. The same can be done with stamping.

Most printers offer sticker-printing services. You can also buy sticker sheets with various pre-cut templates online and print these through your studio printer.

BUROPONY
THE NETHERLANDS

⌃ Cuisson is a one-man cooking army specializing in three fields of expertise: cooking, support, and organization. Each area is represented by a picto-sticker. Cuisson had a small budget and needed a wide range of stationery. By using stickers and placing them on various items, Buropony found a a low-budget means of creating all the required stationery.

CASE STUDY:
REG

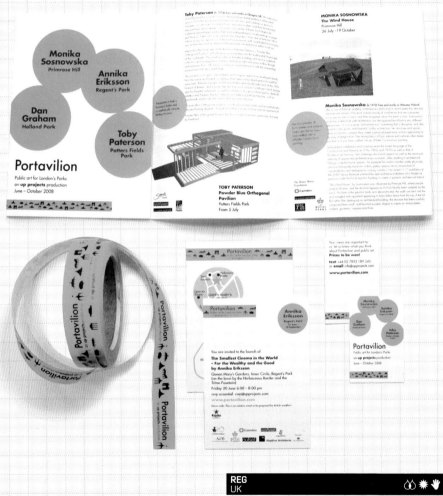

This project, created for UP Projects' Portavilion art exhibition, required a number of printed pieces, from branding to marketing and catalogs.

A cheap, quick, and flexible method of branding was to produce adhesive tape that could be applied to form letterheads, envelopes, and other materials. The main identity was printed one color (black) onto reels of fluorescent-green sticky labels using flexography, which is cheaper than lithography. This formed a sticky tape that could be applied wherever the branding was required. All printed leaflets were created using only two colors (black and fluorescent green), and the catalog cover was printed offset litho, in black only.

The artists' names were printed in-house by laser printer on sheets of pre-cut fluorescent green stickers, then applied to the cover by hand.

Fluorescent colors cannot be achieved using full-color printing methods and can only be achieved using special colors. Flexography and laser-printing processes produced great results for this particular print. Using tape and stickers gave a unique, handcrafted, creative, and original feel to the designs.

REG
UK

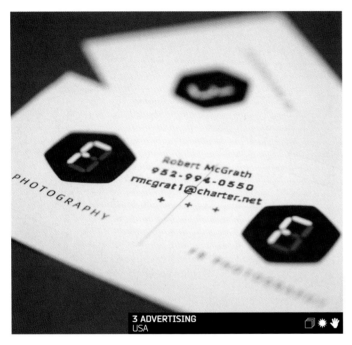

3 ADVERTISING
USA

^ For this business card, 3 Advertising purchased the paper direct from frenchpaper.com and had the card stock cut to size by a local printer. The contact information was applied by rubber stamp, in-house. The logo was printed on strips of paper by another local printer, who then tore the edges of the strips and applied them to all the elements of the package. The process was a little labor-intensive, but well worth the effort.

⌄ Simple, but effective—two spot colors handprinted onto offset board with two rubber stamps.

TURNBULL GREY
UK

SNASK
SWEDEN

^ Working to a small budget, Swedish designers SNASK produced this program/brochure/poster for the Royal School of Theater in Stockholm. The poster was printed in one color, then sent to a different printer for foil blocking. SNASK then took the posters back and screenprinted each one individually. SNASK even managed to borrow a screenprint studio, promising to work out of the studio's office hours. Working between 10pm and 5am, they even baked the posters in a T-shirt oven to speed up the drying, and the finished material was delivered to the client by 9am the next day.

This range of CD covers was created using one spot color backed up with three handmade rubber stamps; each impression produced slightly different results. The card inners were printed on 400gsm American Bristol carton board—a twin board with one smooth and one rough side. Print was applied to the rough side, which is not the usual side for printing. This created a unique and hand-finished aesthetic.

❤ This self-promotional stationery by Italian designers subtitle was printed with silver foil stamping and single-color screenprinting onto a gray/beige paper stock.

BINDING

WPA Pinfold created this self-promotional piece as a highly tactile and desirable company brochure. It was printed in single spot colors onto offset boards and wire-bound.

Binding a document not only holds the job together, it also gives it strength and usability.

A standard format for binding is staple binding. This is simply two vertical staples pushed through the left-hand edge (side staple binding) or spine (saddle staple binding) of the outer jacket and inner pages, then bent over to lock in place. It is not particularly attractive, but it is cheap and it does the job. There are plenty of alternatives for binding, but they are generally more expensive than staple binding, unless, of course you do it yourself. It is possible to hand bind in a number of ways, though this is really only viable for short-run work. It might cost next to nothing on a short production run, but it can make a piece look truly special.

Many things can be used to bind a document, including rubber bands, bulldog clips, and fabric tape. Keep it simple and your alternative approach to binding will make your document truly shine.

WPA PINFOLD
UK

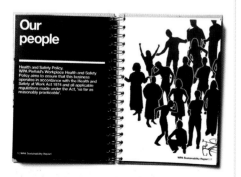

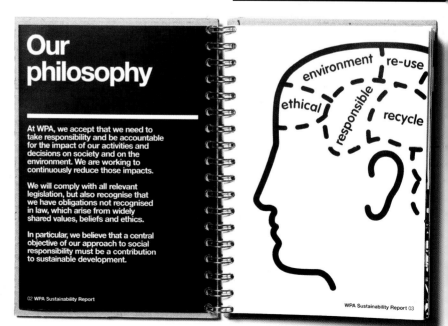

CASE STUDY: STUDIO EMMI

This Concrete Hermit catalog is stylish, innovative, and handbuilt—bound with a paper clip.

The catalog is divided into two sections: the front section contains information about Concrete Hermit along with all the order forms required by prospective buyers. These pages were printed digitally and are updated regularly. The back section works as a catalog – when a page needs updating, it is very easy to remove and update. The paper-clip binding allows a single page to be taken out and renewed at any given time. Overall, this production saved on expensive printing, folding, and binding, saving resources, unnecessary print costs, and time.

STUDIO EMMI
UK

BINDING

Screw-Post

Screw-post binding is very popular. It involves small metal screws with a male and female part locking together to hold a document's pages in position. This finishing can work really well when the outer cover is exceptionally heavy or the document needs to be very strong.

Wire-O Binding

Wire-O binding uses a continuous spine of double loops of wire, which slot into pages that have been punched with rectangular or round holes. The preferred binding method for short-run presentation documents, this can look a little cheap if it is not used carefully, and special equipment is required to punch the holes and close the wires. The advantages of wire binding lie in its strength and flexibility; it allows a document to be folded back on itself, and a book to stay open and flat. Although wire binding takes a fair bit of preparation time (punching holes in the paper—and only a certain number of pages can be punched at one time—lining the pages up correctly, etc.), whole documents can be printed and finished in-house. Back and front covers can be created from anything thin enough to have holes punched through it, offering endless possibilities for giving your document a very particular feel or finish.

Ring Binders

While technically more of a carrying vehicle than a binding, ring binders are another option, but with them lies the danger of your piece looking like a training manual. The advantage of binders is that they protect the document and allow pages to be added very easily, giving you the opportunity to add new material and amend errors.

Comb Binding

This method of binding features a strip of colored plastic with teeth that slot into rectangular holes punched in the leaves of paper, holding them together.

WOLKEN COMMUNICA
USA

> This beautifully produced offset-printed literature for Krekow Jennings features wire binding and screw-post fixing.

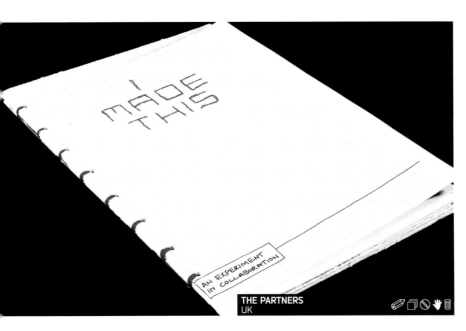

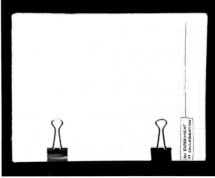

For this catalog and event branding for an exhibition about collaborative art, each visitor was given a huge printed sheet and simple instructions for cutting, folding, and binding. The audience then performed the final act of collaboration by making the exhibition catalog themselves. All other materials, including posters, invitations, and exhibition graphics, carried the same branding as the catalog. Every piece of text was handwritten by the exhibition curator.

THE PARTNERS
UK

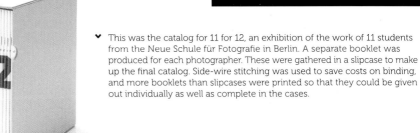

This was the catalog for 11 for 12, an exhibition of the work of 11 students from the Neue Schule für Fotografie in Berlin. A separate booklet was produced for each photographer. These were gathered in a slipcase to make up the final catalog. Side-wire stitching was used to save costs on binding, and more booklets than slipcases were printed so that they could be given out individually as well as complete in the cases.

LITTLE ROOM
CHILE

IN-HOUSE FINISHING

❤ These business cards are supplied to customers perforated and scored so they are easy to fold into a "mini desk Max." Each card is different. They were printed in-house and cut with a perforating cutting blade.

MAX SCHRØDER
NORWAY

HAND-FOLDING

Hand-folding should only really be attempted for short-run work and it is advisable to score documents prior to folding to avoid the paper stock cracking. Generally, it simply isn't worth the time. However, there are occasions when having a piece of print "supplied flat" has its advantages. Folders or dust jackets will generally take up less space when supplied flat, and you can simply make them up as and when you need them, one at a time. If a document has gatefolds or multipage throwouts, these are best folded in by hand. Experiment with hand folding, but beware—if it isn't done properly, the finished piece can look unprofessional and bulky.

THIS IS STUDIO
UK

❮ This show identity for 176 Gallery, which included a publication, show signage, and invitations, was printed single color, and hand finished.

HANDBUILDING

Handmaking goes further than hand finishing and opens up a vast range of possibilities for forms and finishes. Many design studios will produce their own literature, mixing short-run digital inner pages with litho-printed outer covers, bound in-house, and sent out to potential clients as and when required.

Documents can be handmade for many reasons, the most obvious being cost. Handmade work may even include design work that features no external print involvement, relying instead on in-house equipment and copiers. It can cost a great deal of money to print a company brochure and, once produced, it is already out of date as, technically, it is showcasing old work. Commercially bound documents are difficult to update, and what if you move offices? While handmaking a document allows for only a small number to be produced at any one time, that small number of brochures or cards, etc., can be right up to date and feature all the latest work your company has to show.

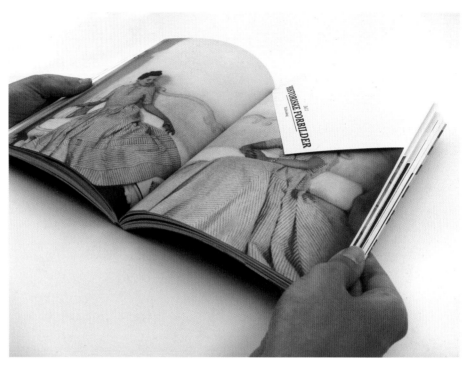

MAX SCHRØDER
NORWAY

∧ Sigrid Søvik's The Master project is about
‹ flexibility in clothes and was inspired by the art of origami. Schrøder included folded pages in his design to physically communicate the idea behind the project. These foldings also surprise the reader and give the impression that this is something special and unusual. The folding was done by hand after printing to keep costs down.

TRAPPED IN SUBURBIA
THE NETHERLANDS

❧ The intention behind these graphics for an exhibition on torture at the museumgoudA was that viewers "discover" the information about each exhibit. This was achieved through the clever use of UV light. Each visitor was given a UV torch on their arrival. In the main room, UV light reveals an explosion of hand-drawn typography on the floor. This was created with the help of a Fab Lab, a public workspace equipped with prototyping and fabrication tools and machines such as 3D printers and laser cutters.

PURPOSE
UK

❧ Purpose created a series of invitations by producing rubber stamps with which to stamp individual packs of Blu-Tack. This tactile invitation was sent out to encourage guests to display and discuss their own work at the event using their very own bit of Blu-Tack.

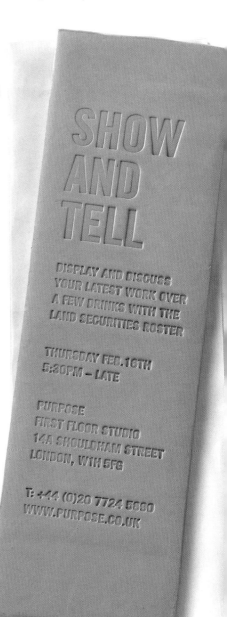

❯ This limited-edition, boxed promotional piece for design house Six contains: two introductory cards, both clear-foiled and printed using Pantone ink on Candy Pink Colorplan from GF Smith; eight project cards on Robert Horne Imagine; and one poster on Pistachio Colorplan. The pack also contains a Picked By Six promo piece presenting highlights from its blog, printed using six colors on a cast-coated stock by Fedrigoni. The modular design of the pack enables Six to add, remove, or replace individual elements. The pack is cost-effective as the contents can be developed or completely refreshed, while the box itself remains constant. Adding the edition to the packs by hand gives a personal touch without any extra cost.

^ The art exhibition Revolver featured six photographers over six shows. The exhibition graphic was a hexagon with the name of each photographer printed on a different side. The subject of the particular show was highlighted by removing the red line of the hexagon outline from that side. The graphic was revolved for each change of show, with a series of acetates clipped into place to reveal the appropriate name. In this way, one set of promotional material was needed rather than six.

ALEXANDER EGGER
AUSTRIA

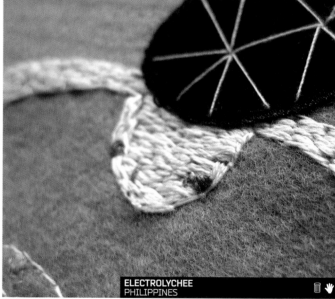

ELECTROLYCHEE
PHILIPPINES

^ Hand-stitched and sewn covers for French
indie band Pas de Printemps, on Philippines
record label Kindassault. One original cover
was handcrafted with stitching, which supplied
the artwork for the remaining covers to be
printed on boards for digipaks.

‹ N76 is a vineyard in Vienna with a small production of exclusive wines.
Every year a new series of designs is applied to the bottles. The logo for the
2007 edition was handsprayed directly onto the bottles and labels.

For this self-promotional Christmas gift, Woodward Design sourced boxes from a local wine-box company, reducing the cost outlay of having a special carrier created just for them. The granola was cooked by Woodward Design, the typography was stamped by hand, and all the stickers and recipe cards were printed digitally in-house and cut by hand.

WOODWARD DESIGN
CANADA

PS.2 ARQUITETURA + DESIGN
BRAZIL

▲ ps.2's self-promotional gift was limited to 300 copies. Each vacuum-sealed pack contains 20 cards, representing 20 different font families. It was all produced in-house by ps.2—they borrowed a vacuum sealer.

Keeping costs down was the priority and the main message for this promotional piece for Laura Santini. A simple single-spot-color sticker was applied by hand.

PURPOSE
UK

FOUND MATERIALS

❤ This stunning set of Christmas cards was produced by Music to send out to friends and clients. Music collected old 12in vinyl records and had the covers foil-blocked and cut down to size by the printer. Each card is different and truly memorable.

MUSIC
UK

The obvious advantage of using existing or found materials is cost. Chances are these materials will be free or at least available at a very low cost. A favorite route is to utilize the leftover materials from a previous job; these have already been paid for, you have them at your disposal, and you can use them to create a smaller run of products for yourself or another client.

Found materials can include offcuts or over-runs, and can be anything from paper to fabric to sheet metal. A good designer can work on just about any material and turn it into a piece of promotional literature. Perhaps forming a good working relationship with your suppliers will allow you to ask, every now and again, for offcuts or samples otherwise destined for the recycling bins.

Another route is to use natural local materials. For example, working on a short run (200 units) of a moving card for a client relocating to new offices two doors along, Traffic Design used the strapline "We are moving just a stone's throw," and sourced small, but beautifully and naturally polished stones from a local beach, tying a stone to each moving card with string. The result was fantastic and achieved at a very small price. But please note, if you take anything from a conservation or protected area, the fines involved may outweigh any money savings.

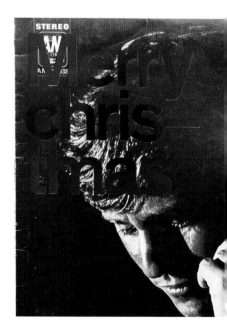

STAYNICE
THE NETHERLANDS

^ For the Here and There exhibition at MU, Eindhoven, staynice created a life-size tree from 11,000 foam "pixels" by using the existing fence as a grid.

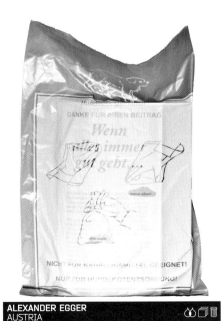

ALEXANDER EGGER
AUSTRIA

‹ Self-promotional Artzine *Wenn alles immer gut geht ...*, limited to a run of 100, was printed in duotone onto Xerox laser copier paper and packed into unused dog-excrement bags.

^ Following on from the Christmas cards on
> the previous page, once Music had used all the
record sleeves, they were left with a large pile
of vinyl records. These they screenprinted and
cut down to size to produce business cards
that are unique and highly effective.

MUSIC
UK

^ Blok and Toxico created the Film Project to
> support independent filmmakers in Brazil.
The identity had to express smart use of
resources, so Blok overprinted the logo on
existing materials, silkscreening every leftover
press approval sheet, found ephemera, etc., that
crossed their paths. A true example of recycling.

BLOK
BRAZIL

Continuing with the "found" theme, pre-owned goods, bankrupt stock, and over-orders can make a fantastic short-run promotional campaign. Occasionally, interesting items appear in ads in local newspapers and in store windows, but the best place to find unusual items, often in bulk, is www.ebay.com. This will usually be an opportunistic purchase. Stumbling across 200 small, empty acrylic display cases could spark the idea of placing an object inside each, and suddenly a short-run promotional concept has been created. One real-world example is 300 small desktop brass bells being purchased for the promotional campaign of a large financial client. To each of these the studio attached a card asking "Ring any bells?" From children's toys to keyrings and clothing, anything can be purchased in large enough quantities to allow for branding and mailing out. Simply keep your eyes and mind open.

WE ARE PUBLIC
UK

Due to the waste paper generated every Christmas, We are Public decided to make use of waste materials for all their future Christmas cards, and to make them valuable in a new way by editioning them. For 2007, they cut 100 sheets of waste card, and stamped and numbered each. For 2008, they found a 1933 copy of Dickens' *A Christmas Carol* that ran to a neat 75 sheets. Each sheet was clipped, numbered, and signed. All Public's Christmas cards are sealed in polybags from a damaged consignment that had been due for destruction. For the 2009 cards, Public repeated the exercise with junk mail.

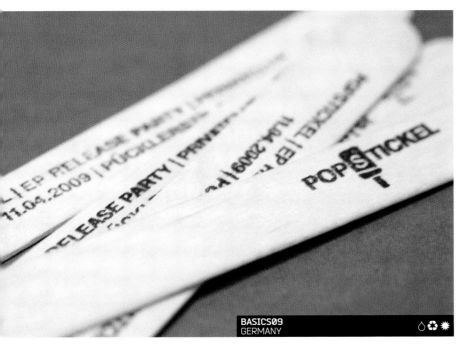

BASICS09
GERMANY

These beautifully printed, single-spot-color sticks were produced to promote band Popstickel. In the end it was actually easier to source wooden tongue spatulae from a pharmacy than it was to get Popsicle sticks!

^ PenguinCube were tasked with helping to reopen many remote mountain
> paths and walkways. It was impossible to create the stone signage system
and carry these up to their locations, so all materials and stencils were
carried into the hills and each concrete slab was mixed, set, dried, and
stencilled in situ.

PENGUINCUBE
LEBANON

LOOKING
GREECE

< In order to cut down on printing costs and to
recycle existing materials, Looking overprinted
copies of newspaper *Athens Voice* in two spot
colors, including silver. These were then cut
down to size and used as the official posters and
brochures for the Green Design Festival in Athens.

CHRISTOF NARDIN
AUSTRIA

^ Debut was a design exhibition held during the
< Vienna Design Week, the venue for which was
a simple market stand. With some dark green
paint and fruit boxes, and a love of typography,
all was transformed.

The goal for this annual report for the Kop Art
spaces in the Netherlands was to produce an
exclusive, high-quality document, but to a very
low budget. The client required only 10 printed
copies. To keep the cost down, staynice printed
all of these in-house on top of posters created
previously for an exhibition. All binding and
folding was finished by hand.

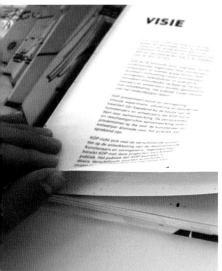

STAYNICE
THE NETHERLANDS

CHAPTER 5: PRE-PRODUCTION & PRINTING

 **Design &**
Print

Graphic Design / Brochures / Leaflets / Prospectuses
Invites / Corporate Branding /Adverts / Flyers
Posters / Business Cards & Stationery / Illustration
Editorial Design / Exhibition Design / Directories
Print Management

To discuss how we can help you with your design or print
needs, please contact Adam or Richard. We look forward
to hearing from you.

OVERVIEW

MICHAEL SEISER
AUSTRIA

‹ Get Rid Off was a hardcore band project in need of a demo tape. The cover had to be something eye-catching to compete with the music this demo tape contained! A handmade paper case, stencils for the graphics, and the use of foam rollers and acrylic paint to "print" the graphics produced a unique look, and an excellent peice of packaging.

Getting the print and production correct is vital for any job, not only to ensure its success and your client's happiness, but also to avoid unexpected and unnecessary costs.

You should always ensure that everything is correct and fully understood before any form of printing commences. In many cases the cost of print and production is greater than the design fees. If you are buying the print on behalf of your client and you bill them for it, you are liable to pay for the reprint if anything goes wrong. Even asking the client to sign off on a final proof isn't insurance against a job coming back wrong. Having to pay for a reprint can be hugely expensive, and just as bad is receiving a bill that exceeds the quote supplied and for which you must make up the difference from your own design fees. This happens more often than you would think.

It is crucial that you put together a short-list of printers suitable for a specific project. Small printers with a two-color press only will not be suitable for a large-run, four-color brochure. It simply won't be cost-effective to produce a printed job run through a two-color press twice. The reverse applies for short-run spot-color work. Is it really viable to give this to a large printing company and pay for a huge press to produce a small-run postcard? Get at least three quotes in and pick the best quote for the job. Remember that the best quote is not always the cheapest—you get what you pay for.

Beware hidden costs. Have you told the printer exactly what you are looking for? If you are not clear and precise with your quote request, you will be charged more. Insist that your quote includes delivery, but be honest about where it is to be delivered to. Printers will usually do one local "drop" free, but if you require delivery to a number of destinations they will charge a fee. Check that your artwork is correct and that you have included all fonts and high-resolution images. You will be charged if photo manipulation is required. Does the job need a specific cutter for pages or pockets cut to a special shape? Does it need die-cuts to hold business cards? Are there large areas of flat color that will need a sealer varnish to prevent ink rubbing off onto facing pages? Is it printed onto heavy board (300gsm and up) that will crack when scored and folded? If so, you will need to budget for a matte-lamination plastic coating.

Scoring is an additional finishing and will therefore incur an extra charge. If it's a large print run, this can add quite a chunk to the final bill. If you keep the paper weight under about 175gsm, it can usually be folded without scoring, which will save you a lot of money.

Can you print similar jobs at the same time, even if they are for different clients? Substantial savings can be made in this way, especially if they have the same specifications and use the same paper stock. In this case they can be printed up on sheets together, saving up to a third of the cost of printing both separately. Encourage your client to produce print in batches rather than one project at a time.

Do you really need to approve printed paper sheets or test proofs prior to the full run commencing? Save money and time (on smaller, simple print jobs) by approving an online electronic PDF sent to you by e-mail and viewed on-screen. Make sure your printer knows you don't need to see paper proofs, and save on this additional cost.

Another possible opportunity to save on print fees is to be flexible with delivery times. Is the job urgent? Can it be printed in between other jobs? It's worth asking. If the usual turnaround time is five days, will they reduce the cost for allowing 10 days? Is there a discount for immediate payment/cash on delivery?

When it comes to print buying, you will benefit from experience. The more you place, the more you learn about how to save money. Most printers will be helpful and on your side; after all, they will want you to come back again. Give them as much information as possible along with good artwork for the project you want printed, and savings can be made. Try to form a good relationship with several print suppliers and they should advise you on the most cost-effective way to produce your project.

TIP

When printing stationery, always make sure you print compliments slips and letterheads together, on the same stock. The printer will double these up onto larger sheets and cut down. Insist on a single cost to print and supply both. By having the compliments slip the same width as the letterhead and one-third the height, the slips can be printed three-up with the letterheads. This creates a ratio of 1 to 3, so a good way of quoting stationery is to ask for 1,000 letterheads supplied with 3,000 compliments slips, or 2,000 with 6,000, and so on. Don't put the words "with compliments" on the compliments slips; without this your client can use them for everything from address labels on envelopes to storage-box labels.

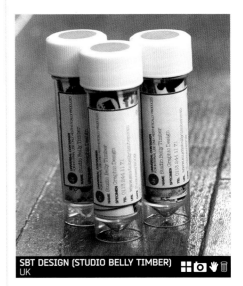

This self-promotional work, headed "A sample of our work," included mini folios placed in hospital urine-sample vessels with pharmacy-style labels applied by hand.

SBT DESIGN (STUDIO BELLY TIMBER)
UK

BEWARE!

It is usually free to deliver to one local destination, but if you ask for multiple destinations you will be expected to pay for this. You may also have to pay handling fees for splitting up the print run and boxing it up in individual quantities or types, ready for delivery. Remember to agree this prior to any print work starting. Beware of producing promotional merchandise, giveaways, branded toys, etc., where the quote states "Delivery costs to be confirmed." Confirm this before agreeing anything. Promotional items and plastics may be purchased in your own area, but manufactured in another country. This can lead to import duty, heavy charges for shipping or flying goods in, long delivery times, etc. It's not unusual for these delivery fees to add hundreds to the cost—a cost that may have to be covered by you.

PRODUCING YOUR OWN PRINT

MUSTARD UP
UK

You will never get as good a quality producing print in-house as you will get from a conventional printer (unless you happen to have a full-color Heidelberg litho press at your disposal), but in many cases that's the whole point.

Handmade, -bound and -constructed merchandise will have the cache of a unique limited edition. Handbuilt brochures from digital printouts can look like one-off specials, making the recipient feel as though it was made just for them. Don't be over-complex with your construction—the fewer stages required the better—and remember to keep quantities low. It may well take a week to produce 300 handbuilt brochures, and that is a week of lost revenue. It's not worth it. Taking two hours to produce a handful of brochures is much more practical.

Mix and match your finishes. Perhaps you can make every brochure different. Can you order up quality card from a paper mill as samples, free of charge, then cut these down to size and add in/on your own digital prints?

You can also mix mass-produced print with in-house hand finishing. This is an excellent way to control the overall content, save money, and still be able to produce short-run material.

Don't try to replicate the precise finishing of a professional printer—it won't work— but don't send out something that looks like it was produced by a five-year-old (unless, of course, that's the point). You may not always get it right, but experiment. Trial and error works best when you are producing your own material.

^ MUSTARD UP were commissioned by Underdogs to produce 150 invitations to celebrate the launch of their new recording studio. Recycled card from a previous project was used and cut with a scalpel. The assembly was done by hand over a period of 15 hours, by five people!

FABRICE PRAEGER
FRANCE

This press release to the music industry took the form of an identity kit, containing several pieces of "evidence," all neatly labeled.

BUROPONY didn't have a lot of money to spend on an identity when they started up. This idea is based on the patterns worn by jockeys during a horse race. BUROPONY designed a two-color grid (with a third color printed as a base color). By printing one spot color and manually enriching all items with markers and spray cans, they created a flexible identity that stands out and is a great conversation piece for the agency.

BUROPONY
THE NETHERLANDS

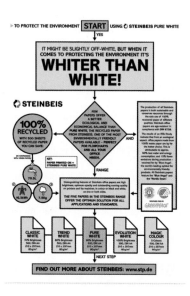

STOCKS TAYLOR BENSON
UK

‹
˅ The finished promotional pieces for this new range of 100% recycled papers were simply photocopied onto the actual stock in-house, by the client's marketing team, as required. This meant that one or all of the papers in the range could be printed as and when they were needed, eliminating the need for excessive print runs and paper wastage.

›
˅ The aim of this promotional box was to raise funds for the Brazilian film project *Mirror and Shadows*. Since they did not have much money to work with, Blok decided to divide the project into two. The outer box and black-and-white cards were beautifully printed on letterpress. The four-color inside image cards were printed digitally in-house by Blok and trimmed at the studio by the designers themselves.

BLOK
BRAZIL

∧ For this CD sleeve Landland bought in
> pre-die-cut, unfolded, unprinted sleeves from
a local printer. The rest of the components were
simply photocopied in-house or at local copy
shops. Everything was printed and assembled
in-house by the designers.

LANDLAND
USA

EDHV
THE NETHERLANDS

^ Edhv produced a magazine in just four days. There were six proposed cover designs, so, in true eccentric style, all six were screenprinted, one on top of the other. The inner pages were digitally printed, hole-punched, and bound by hand. A total of 500 were produced.

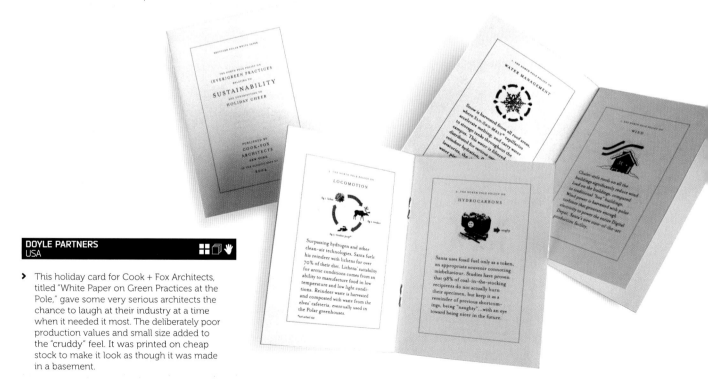

DOYLE PARTNERS
USA

> This holiday card for Cook + Fox Architects, titled "White Paper on Green Practices at the Pole," gave some very serious architects the chance to laugh at their industry at a time when it needed it most. The deliberately poor production values and small size added to the "cruddy" feel. It was printed on cheap stock to make it look as though it was made in a basement.

"By an object, I mean anything that we can think, i.e. anything we can talk about."

Un-
Objectivity

ON MEANINGLESSNESS

This self-initiated project, a little art book designed in collaboration with the designer's wife Ariadne Binderl, was printed on recycled paper with minimal use of color. All printing was done using an ink-jet printer with colored paper for special pages and the cover.

ALEX LINS
BRAZIL

Most of this CD packaging for band Decembers Architects was printed in a basement, with some printed at a local copy shop. The sleeves were supplied overprinted and die-cut, for assembly by hand.

LANDLAND
USA

CHAPTER 6:
RESOURCES

GIVE UP ART
UK

SUMMARY OF SOURCES

FONT-RELATED SITES

www.007fonts.com
www.1001freefonts.com
www.1-800-fonts.com
www.abstractfonts.com
www.acidfonts.com
www.bvfonts.com
www.dafont.com
www.fontface.com
www.fontfreak.com/pre.htm
www.fontifier.com
www.fontlab.com
www.fontsearchengine.com
www.fontsforflash.com
www.fontstruct.fontshop.com
www.fontsy.com
www.highfonts.com
www.jabroo.com
www.searchfreefonts.com
www.typenow.net
www.urbanfonts.com
www.webfxmall.com/fonts

IMAGE SITES

www.123rf.com
www.acclaimimages.com
www.alamy.com
www.bigstockphoto.com
www.canstockphoto.com
www.cepolina.com
www.corbis.com
www.crestock.com
www.dreamstime.com
www.easystockphotos.com
www.en.fotolia.com
www.everystockphoto.com
www.flickr.com
www.fotosearch.co.uk
www.freedigitalphotos.net
www.freefoto.com
www.freeimages.co.uk
www.freemediagoo.com
www.freephotosbank.com
www.freepixels.com
www.freerangestock.com
www.freestockphotos.com
www.gettyimages.com
www.imageafter.com
www.inmagine.com
www.istockphoto.com
www.jupiterimages.co.uk
www.morguefile.com
www.openphoto.net
www.photogen.com
www.photorack.net
www.photos.com
www.photospin.com
www.pixmac.com
www.public-domain-photos.com
www.punchstock.co.uk
www.shutterstock.com
www.stockphotoasia.com
www.stockvault.net
www.stockxpert.com
www.sxc.hu
www.texturewarehouse.com
www.unprofound.com

BLOGS/FORUMS & INSPIRATION

www.acejet170.typepad.com
www.aisleone.net
www.bibliodyssey.blogspot.com
www.bitique.co.uk
www.booooooom.com
www.buamai.com
www.butdoesitfloat.com
www.cpluv.com
www.creativeoutput.net/blog
www.design21sdn.com
www.designobserver.com
www.dezeen.com
www.dirtymouse.co.uk
www.dropular.net
www.ffffound.com
www.fleuron.com
www.formfiftyfive.com
www.fubiz.net
www.heavyeyes.net
www.grafikcache.com
www.grainedit.com
www.graphichug.com
www.hipyoungthing.com
www.itsnicethat.com
www.manystuff.org
www.modernthought.co.uk
www.nolegacy.com
www.original-linkage.blogspot.com
www.reformrevolution.com
www.septemberindustry.co.uk
www.somuchpileup.blogspot.com
www.swisslegacy.com
www.thedieline.com
www.thegridsystem.org
www.the-refined.com
www.thestrangeattractor.net
www.typojungle.net
www.underconsideration.com/brandnew
www.welcometohr.com
www.yayeveryday.com
www.ypeish.com

PAPER MILLS/SUPPLIERS

www.abcpaper.in
www.abitibibowater.com
www.adpaper.ae
www.ahlstrom.com
www.akasan.com.tr
www.alamigeon.com
www.alceicl.com
www.amcor.com
www.andhrapaper.com
www.appletoncoated.com
www.arapepco.com
www.arcticpaper.com
www.arjowiggins.com
www.asiapaper.co.kr
www.australianpaper.com.au
www.awusa.com
www.aylesford-newsprint.co.uk
www.bollorethinpapers.com
www.bruecherpapier.de
www.buchmannkarton.de
www.burgogroup.it
www.canson-us.com
www.cartieradelchiese.it
www.cartieradelladda.com
www.cartieradigalliera.com
www.cartieragiorgione.com
www.cartotecnicarossi.it
www.centurypaper.com.pk
www.champaper.com
www.chuetsu-pulp.co.jp
www.clearwaterpaper.com
www.clc.com.tw
www.cmpc.cl
www.coldenhove.com
www.copamex.com
www.cqzzyjy.com
www.crane.se
www.cropper.com
www.curtisfinepapers.com
www.cvg.nl
www.daehanpaper.co.kr
www.daio-paper.co.jp
www.dalumpapir.dk
www.domtar.com

www.dongilpaper.co.kr
www.doubleapaper.com
www.drewsen.com
www.emin-leydier.com
www.environmentalbychoice.com
www.fedrigoni.com
www.fibermark.com
www.fibria.com.br
www.flambeauriverpapers.com
www.fukuyama-paper.jp
www.galgo.com
www.gardacartiere.it
www.garnettpapers.com
www.gfsmith.com
www.glommapapp.no
www.gruppocordenons.com
www.grycksbopaper.com
www.guyennepapier.fr
www.hadera-paper.co.il
www.hanchangpaper.co.kr
www.heinzelgroup.com
www.horizon.ee
www.hyogoseishi.com
www.iggesundpaperboard.com
www.internationalpaper.com
www.jass.de
www.jssd.de
www.khannapaper.com
www.koehlerpaper.com
www.koehlerpappen.de
www.korsnas.com
www.kruger.com
www.lanapapier.fr
www.lucart.it
www.mohawkpaper.com
www.mondigroup.com
www.mpm.com
www.m-real.com
www.myllykoski.com
www.nordic-paper.com
www.okayamaseishi.co.jp
www.paperonweb.com
www.petrocart.ro
www.sappi.com

www.scheufelen.com
ww.smartpapers.com
www.smurfitkappa.com
www.sniace.com
www.strathconapaper.com
www.stregis.co.uk
www.sunpapercompany.com
www.suomenkuitulevy.fi
www.sypaper.co.kr
www.thesharmagroup.com
www.tppc.com.tw
www.tullis-russell.co.uk
www.utzenstorf-papier.ch
www.vignaletto.com
www.visy.com.au
www.weyerhaeuser.com
www.zanders.de
www.zeritis.gr

VECTOR ILLUSTRATIONS

www.123freevectors.com
www.coolvectors.com
www.createsk8.com
www.dezignus.com
www.flavafx.com
www.flickr.com
www.freevectors.net
www.istockphoto.com
www.keepdesigning.com
www.qvectors.com
www.vecteezy.com
www.vector4free.com
www.vectorart.org
www.vector-art.blogspot.com
www.vectorjungle.com
www.vectorportal.com
www.vectorvalley.com
www.vectorvault.com
www.vectorwallpapers.net
www.veeqi.com
www.vintagevectors.com

GLOSSARY

PRINTING

bitmap
A generic style of computer-originated typeface, constructed pixel by pixel. The term is also used to describe the pixelation of a digital image.

bleed
The term used to refer to an element printed beyond the trimmed edge of the page, allowing the image, rule, or type to extend to the very edge of the printed page.

CMYK
Stands for cyan, magenta, yellow, and key (black). These primary ink colors are combined on a press to produce a full range of color. Also known as full- or four-color printing.

digital printing
The reproduction of digital images on a physical surface, such as photographic paper, film, cloth, or plastic, etc.

duotone
A halftone made of two colors; two colors are printed together to make an image richer and denser in color.

engraving/etched plates
Printing method using a metal plate with an image cut or acid-etched into its surface.

halftone
A process used to reproduce an illustration, which involves breaking it up into small dots of different densities to simulate a full tonal range.

holography
Using lasers to overlay embossed images onto film, then paper to produce the effect of a 3D image.

inks (specials, metallics, fluorescents)
Most mass-produced books are printed using lithographic inks. As a rule, full-color printing is achieved through combining the four process colors (cyan, magenta, yellow, and black), however, additional "special" inks can also be used to produce distinctive results.

letterpress
A traditional method of printing type, using a series of metal stamps with individual letters cast on the surface. The printed sheet is more tactile than that produced by conventional offset lithographic printing because the type is debossed into the surface.

offset lithography
The standard format of printing by which an image on a plate is offset to a rubber blanket cylinder, which, in turn, transfers the image to a sheet of paper.

raster imaging
An alternative method of halftone screening using an electron beam. It creates complex, irregular patterns of very fine dots and produces higher-quality images and color work than conventional CMYK litho.

reversed type
Letters are left unprinted with the surrounding area printed to allow the color of the stock to show through as type.

RGB
Stands for red, green, and blue, the three primary colors used on-screen to generate a full spectrum of color.

screenprinting
The method of printing by which ink is forced through a stencil glued to a mesh or screen. Also referred to as silkscreening or serigraphy.

spot color
A special color not generated by the four-color process method, often sourced from the Pantone swatch range.

vignette
A graduated tint by which one color fades into another color or white.

woodblock/rubber die
Letters carved in pieces of wood or rubber to be relief-printed: similar to letterpress.

FOLDING

concertina fold
Pages folded in a zigzag manner, like the bellows of a concertina. The paper can be extended to its full length with a single pull. Also known as fan or accordion folding.

cross-fold
A printed page is folded, then turned over and folded in the opposite direction to give multiple folds similar to a map.

French fold
The method of folding a page in half and binding along the open edges.

gatefold
The outer edges of the page are folded inward to meet the gutter, without overlapping. Often used on center-page spreads to create impact.

perforated fold
Printing sheets are perforated prior to folding down to the page size; this allows French-fold pages to be torn open easily.

roll fold
A long sheet of paper is folded into panels or pages starting from the far right, with each subsequent panel folded back toward the left. Effectively, it is rolled back around itself.

scoring
Marking/impressing the fold line on paper. This is required on heavier paper (175–200gsm and above) to allow clean folding.

throw-out
A page bigger than the finished size of the document is folded in on itself to fit within the document. This allows for bigger pages than those of standard sizes.

MATERIALS

cast-coated
Paper that has a very high-quality, high-gloss surface on one side, while the reverse remains matte and uncoated. Achieved by pressing the paper against a metal drum while the clay coating is still wet.

coated stock
A smooth, hard-surfaced paper good for reproducing halftone images. It is created by coating the surface with china clay.

cover/bookbinding board
A dense, coated fiberboard used for the covers of casebound books.

injection molding
The process used to produce large quantities of identical plastic items. It uses high-impact polystyrenes (HIPS).

Kraft paper
Strong paper made from unbleached wood pulp. This is often used for paper bags and giftwrap due to its strength.

Perspex
A trade name for Polymethylmethacrylate. It is a tough plastic, first produced in 1930 and widely used for advertising signs and protective shields. Also manufactured under the names Plexiglas, Lucite, Acrylite, and Rophlex.

polypropylene
A flexible plastic sheet available in many different colors, including clear and frosted.

pulpboard
Pulpboard is very thick with a rough, recycled feel. A highly absorbent, flexible, and resilient sheet that allows ink to soak into it, giving a very rustic feel.

ream
Five hundred sheets of any type of paper.

signature
A printed sheet folded at least once to become part of a printed document. Signatures are also made up in sets of four, eight, sixteen, etc.

simulator paper
A thin, translucent paper, more commonly known as tracing paper.

stock
The paper or other material on which a job is printed.

translucent paper
An almost see-through/transparent stock that allows some light through, making it perfect for overlays.

uncoated stock
Paper not coated with clay, which has a rougher surface than coated paper. Because of this it is both bulkier and more opaque.

BINDING

binding tape
Tape or other material that binds the spine of a book to protect the edges and allow for easy opening.

burstbound
The pages of a document are gathered, but not sewn. Instead, the folded edges are perforated and glue is inserted into these perforations.

casebound
Glue is used to hold sections of pages (signatures) to a case made of thick board, which is bound in plastic, fabric, or leather.

channel binding
A mechanical binding system that uses a metal U-channel built into a one-piece cover. No punching or gluing is required. A number of systems allow for a limited debinding of documents.

Japanese binding
Thread is bound from the back to the front of the book, around the outside edge of the spine. Used primarily for binding loose sheets.

perfect binding
Pages are glued to the cover and held together with a strip of adhesive, giving the spine of the brochure a completely flat finish.

saddle-stitching
The standard method of binding for printed literature: pages are secured with stitches or staples placed through the centerfold of nested signatures.

screw-post binding
Pages are held together with bolts inserted through drilled holes and fixed on the reverse with a post.

side stitching
Pages are stapled and bound together along one edge. Also known as sidewire.

Singer-sewn binding
Binding by sewing along the centerfold of a document with an industrial version of the sewing machine.

wire/comb binding
The teeth of a plastic comb or thin metal wire are inserted through holes on a stack of paper, locking the pages into the binding mechanism.

FINISHING

debossing
A surface pattern is pressed into paper or material to leave a recessed impression.

die-cut
The method by which a decorative shape is cut from a page. It is created using a die which has a sharp steel edge constructed to cut the exact shape.

embossing
As debossing, but produces a raised impression instead of a recessed one. Blind embossing is embossing without foil or ink.

engraving
Printing method using a metal plate with an image cut into its surface to hold ink, which is then pressed onto the paper.

foil blocking
A foil and a heated die are brought together and stamped onto paper to form a printed impression.

forme cut
A die forme is used to cut a document to a nonstandard shape.

gloss metallic foil
As for foil blocking, but a metallic foil is used with a gloss printed directly on top.

hand finishing
Anything that can't be produced by machinery requires hand finishing, from folding in scored pages and throw-outs to adding inserts or binding a document.

in-line sealing
During the printing process, a thin varnish is applied to large areas of printed material instead of an extra color, sealing the page to avoid the ink rubbing off onto the opposite page. Often applied as a fifth color during the CMYK printing process.

kiss-cut
Similar to die-cutting, but does not pass right through the sheet. Mostly used for making sticker sheets where the backing paper must remain intact.

lamination
The application of a protective plastic film over the printed surface or sheet.

laser die-cut
A very precise method of cutting, this can cope with far more intricate shapes than conventional die-cutting.

laser etching
Using this process, patterns or text can be written in high resolution and transferred to the underlying material via reactive ion etching.

pin perforations
Small holes made by puncturing the surface of the paper with pins. Mostly used for cutting long series of holes so that paper can be torn more easily.

ram punch
A ram punch, or punch press, is a machine tool used for cutting precise shapes in metal, card, or paper. It is generally used for heavier card or large quantities of paper/card.

thermography
A relief effect created by dusting a special powder onto a printed image while still wet, then passing the sheet through a heating device.

UV varnish
A liquid varnish applied and then heat-cured with ultraviolet light, resulting in a tough, durable, and glossy finish.

CONTRIBUTORS

INDEX